THE
SAILORS' SNUG HARBOR

D1567700

Augustus Saint Gaudens created the giant bronze statue of the founder of Sailors' Snug Harbor, Captain Robert Richard Randall, in 1878. Since 1976, it has faced the Harbor's new home for aged sailors in Sea Level, North Carolina. A bronze copy stands on the original marble pedestal at the old Staten Island campus.

GERALD J. BARRY

THE
SAILORS' SNUG HARBOR
❧ A HISTORY ❧

1 8 0 1
~
2 0 0 1

FORDHAM UNIVERSITY PRESS

NEW YORK

2000

ISBN: 0-8232-2072-9 (hardcover)

ISBN: 0-8232-2073-7 (paper)

Library of Congress Cataloging-in-Publication Data

Barry, Gerald J.

The Sailors' Snug Harbor: A History/Gerald J. Barry.—1st ed.

   p. cm.

Includes bibliographical references and index.

ISBN: 0-8232-2072-9 (hardcover)—ISBN: 0-8232-2073-7 (paper)

1. Sailors' Snug Harbor (Institution) 2. Merchant seamen—Institutional care—New York (State) 3. Merchant seamen—Institutional care—North Carolina. I. Title.

VK220 .B37 2000

362.85'85'0883875—dc21

00-044246

Typesetting and design by Christina Rubin

Printed in the United States of America

00 01 02 03 04 5 4 3 2 1

First Edition

To Susie and James

TABLE OF CONTENTS

ACKNOWLEDGMENTS

This book could not have been written without the support of the trustees of The Sailors' Snug Harbor. But the greatest debt is owed to Captain Leo Kraszeski, who encouraged me in every way and corrected me when I went astray without attempting to influence my editorial view. Captain Kraszeski, who is a trustee, was governor and executive director of the Harbor from June 1969 to June 1987. In addition, he is first vice president of The Marine Society of the City of New York. We met in 1995 when I wrote a history of the society for its 225th anniversary.

The bulk of Harbor archives are deposited in the Stephen B. Luce Library at the Maritime College of the State University of New York in Fort Schuyler, Bronx, New York. Original copies of the minutes of trustee meetings from 1806 to the present are kept at the Harbor institution in Sea Level, North Carolina.

Richard Corson, director of the Luce Library, arranged to acquire two sets of records in 1976 when the Harbor was preparing to move to North Carolina. The first—contained in three large sea chests stored in the attic of the administration building in Staten Island—deal mainly with the daily management of the Harbor from its opening in 1833 to the 1920s and 1930s. Letters from residents or inmates, as they were called in earlier days, along with those from governors and comptrollers and detailed account books kept by butcher, baker, farmer, carpenter, engineer, library, and visitor registers provide, collectively, a fairly complete picture of life at the Harbor during various periods. The Fort Schuyler files also contain biographical data about Thomas Randall, including records sent to the trustees in 1908 by the chamber of commerce—one of the organizations that he helped to found.

The second group of records was maintained by the Harbor's Manhattan office on Greene Street. Basically, these records concern the physical maintenance of the Staten Island facility, Manhattan property leases, and the administration of the Trust. Included are the Randall wills and copies of deeds pertaining to the "Minto Farm," which became Sailors' Snug Harbor.

In the early 1930s, Don C. Seitz wrote "A History of Captain Robert Richard Randall's Foundation for the Toilers of the Sea." The unpublished manuscript ran to 366 double-spaced, typewritten pages. Included in those easy-to-read pages were most of the significant events reported in the handwritten minutes of a century's worth of trustee meetings plus relevant press clippings and other background notes. Thank you, Doctor Seitz. Thanks also to Norman Brouwer, curator of ships and maritime historian at the South Street Seaport Museum; to the librarians and photo-researchers at the New-York Historical Society, the Museum of the City of New York, and the map room and the genealogical and local history division of the New York Public Library; and to the helping hands at Fort Schuyler, Sea Level, and the Snug Harbor Cultural Center. A special thank you to Dr. Mary Beatrice Schulte of Fordham University Press for editorial advice.

INTRODUCTION

After serving on American Vessels for a period of time extending over forty years leading the life of an Ocean Slave on many ships which were veritable "floating hells" robbed, beaten and starved by tyrant Captains and "Bucko" mates, abused, plundered and Shanghaied by shipping crimps on land, until a sailor's life on most American ships was naught but a hell on earth, without one ray of hope to gladden him on his way through life's journey, but the beacon that shone forth from Randall's Noble Legacy, Sailors Snug Harbor.

Frank Waters, Snug Harbor resident, February 28, 1918

The Randall referred to in Waters's lament is Robert Richard Randall—son of Thomas Randall, privateer, Revolutionary War patriot, and entrepreneur who created the family fortune. Robert Richard, a bachelor of about 50 years, had lived the life of a country gentleman on the Randall farm before his death on June 5, 1801, four days after signing a remarkable will. It provided that his mansion and 21-acre farm be used to maintain and support "aged, decrepit, and worn-out sailors." The will boldly ordered that this "Sailors' Snug Harbor" be governed "forever" by eight of New York's most important men—the chancellor of the state, the mayor and recorder of the city, the head of the chamber of commerce, the senior ministers of the Episcopal and Presbyterian churches, and the president and vice president of The Marine Society (at the time New York's most prestigious organization).

Every one of these soon-to-be trustees accepted the terms of the will, even though its vision seemed far larger than the $15,000 value of the estate. Nearly five years passed before DeWitt Clinton, mayor and president of the board of trustees, prevailed upon a reluctant state legislature to approve the Act of Incorporation for Sailors' Snug Harbor.

As the 1820s approached, New York was pulling ahead of Philadelphia and Boston as the center of American commerce and finance. Wealthy businessmen and their families abandoned the noisy, newly congested Battery and Wall Street neighborhood for rustic Bleecker and Bond Streets. The uptown march of Broadway had stalled a few blocks farther on at a white fence marking the boundary of the Randall farm, which only recently had been two miles north of the city proper.

With land values soaring, the trustees asked the legislature to modify Randall's will so that Sailors' Snug Harbor could be built somewhere other than the farm. Their petition was approved, and the farm was subdivided into 253 leasehold lots covering most of the 10 square city blocks between what would become Fourth and Fifth Avenues, Waverly Place, and Tenth Street.

Before a decision could be made on a new site for the old sailors' home, petitioners claiming to be collateral heirs of the Randalls brought legal suits against the trustees to challenge the will. One of the litigants, the New York–born Anglican Bishop of Nova Scotia, John Inglis, fought all the way to the U.S. Supreme Court where he was represented by the formidable Daniel Webster. On January 2, 1830, the Court voted three to two in favor of the will. Almost three decades after Captain Randall wrote his will, the trustees were free to find a new location for the seamen's home and to get on with the business of becoming an important landlord to New Yorkers.

In May 1831, the trustees purchased a 130-acre farm overlooking Upper New York Bay and the Kill Van Kull on Staten Island for $10,000. They chose young architect Minard Lafever to design a building that would accommodate 200 seamen with "the necessary offices, kitchen, storerooms, etc." The central building in a complex of what would be a row of five Greek Revival–style dormitories opened on August 1,

1833. Thirty-seven retired seamen attended the opening ceremonies as the first resident-beneficiaries of Randall's will.

Year by year, buildings were added until there were 55 major structures. The Harbor produced its own electricity and steam; grew its own food; had its own water supply; and included a church, cemetery, hospital, theater, and library on the premises. At the opening of the twentieth century, more than 1,000 old sailors were in residence.

Income from the one-time Randall farm in Manhattan, whose leased lots were creating a wealthy residential neighborhood, paid for all the construction and care on Staten Island. Leases for lots fronting on Broadway and the Bowery, each 25 feet wide and 100 feet deep, were auctioned at the Tontine Coffee House beginning in February 1827. Annual rents ranged from $130 to $150 for leases of 21 years. Business was slow until the U.S. Supreme Court cleared the way for the trustees to implement the will.

A full block of Harbor property from Fifth Avenue to University Place faced a recently vacated potters field when Philip Hone became mayor and president of the Sailors' Snug Harbor Board of Trustees. Rather than divide the 12-acre open field into building lots that the city would sell, Hone had the land upgraded and enlarged into a military parade ground named for George Washington. It was soon to become Washington Square Park and a desirable residential neighborhood.

In 1832, three socially prominent businessmen leased the Washington Square North property from Sailors' Snug Harbor and built a unified row of 13 Greek Revival mansions. Long before zoning regulations, the trustees and their lessees agreed upon a set of restrictions designed to protect against nuisances and to attract wealthy residents.

"The Row" was home to six of the founders of New York University (NYU), whose grand Gothic Revival building opened on the east side of Washington Square in 1835. Five years later, the South Dutch Reformed Church opened immediately below NYU. Its Gothic Revival towers complemented those of its neighbor and gave the east side of the square a romantic skyline. Long rows of brick residences, handsome but more modest than their northerly neighbors, lined the south and west sides of the park. Beyond the square, families of merchants, brokers, lawyers, publishers, physicians, and ministers turned the old Randall farmland into an upper-class neighborhood.

By the time the Harbor's 21-year leases began to come up for renewal in the 1850s, hotels, restaurants, shops, and music halls were replacing residences along Broadway. Overshadowing all the change was the trustees' agreement to lease 29 lots between Broadway, Fourth Avenue, Ninth Street, and Tenth Street to Alexander Turney Stewart for America's first true department store. A. T. Stewart's splendid, five-floor store employed 500 clerks and cashiers and was visited daily by as many as 15,000 shoppers, mostly women. Stewart's store was the anchor of a shopping area that became known as "Ladies Mile."

At the same time, the general area around Astor Place and Washington Square earned the sobriquet "Athenaeum Quarter" because of its cluster of libraries, bookstores, art galleries, churches, the Astor Place Opera House, NYU, and the Cooper Union for the Advancement of Science and Art.

The old residents of the Harbor itself, veterans of hard and dangerous lives at sea, had little in common with their benefactors in Manhattan who looked upon them as rogues and rascals. The notoriety was often well earned, because life at sea and ashore had done little to prepare seamen for polite society. Discipline aboard ship was enforced by leather lash. On land, the wages of the solitary sailor were fair game for crimps and whores and rum mills.

It was well into the nineteenth century before the harsh social climate in which mariners had always lived began to soften. Congress banned flogging and seriously undercut the crimping business. The Social Security Act of 1933 and the formation of powerful maritime unions brought old-age and unemployment insurance, along with welfare and pension plans to the seamen. With these amenities, reports of drunkenness among sailors began to diminish.

As for the Sailors' Snug Harbor itself, the depression years were harsh. Even when the facility's maintenance needs were ignored, income barely covered expenses because so many Manhattan tenants were unable to pay their rent. Deferred maintenance continued during World War II and, as a result, Harbor properties suffered major deterioration.

Beginning in 1950, as part of a "modernization and improvement plan," two dozen buildings on the Staten Island property were bulldozed. Next on the destruction list were the Greek Revival dormitories, which were to be replaced by a 120-bed modern infirmary mandated by the New York State Department of Health. At this point, the city's new Landmarks Preservation Commission stepped in. On October 14,

1965, at its first designation hearing, the commission landmarked and saved the old dormitories. Unable to satisfy both state and city agencies, the trustees claimed they had no choice but to leave Staten Island.

Property for a new institution for the old sailors was found in Sea Level, North Carolina, down the road from a hospital recently taken over by the Duke University Medical Center. Citing the proximity of Duke's hospital to the new site, the New York Surrogate Court approved relocation of Sailor's Snug Harbor.

New York Mayor John Lindsay, in June 1973, announced a plan to turn the Greek Revival buildings and 80 acres of Harbor land into a national showplace of culture and education. The purchase price was $9.7 million. The Snug Harbor Cultural Center, well worth a visit, remains a work in progress. The Manhattan leaseholds were sold for $24.5 million to be held in perpetuity by the Randall Endowment, a trust fund that will continue to support "aged, decrepit, and worn out sailors."

The Harbor's Sea Level facility, perhaps the finest retirement facility in the United States, opened in June 1976 with private quarters for 120 retired mariners. In recent years, the comfortable quarters have been only three-fourths full. Rooms are empty because of several major changes in maritime culture:

• Two-thirds of the men and women eligible for admission to the Harbor are married and have ties to a specific area.
• Because of work-schedule changes in the maritime industry, well-paid, able-bodied seamen spend almost as much time with their families as they do at sea.
• Adequate health care is available throughout the country, eliminating the need for retired sailors to collect in a central location.

In December 1996, the New York Surrogate Court granted the trustees permission to supplement the income of eligible seamen who need help but prefer to live somewhere other than Sea Level. Eventually, this program will result in the withdrawal of the Harbor from the Sea Level facility. But with this change, the Randall Endowment will be able to help hundreds of mariners rather than a few score. The program will be run by a small staff in New York City.

A Note About Street Names

In the 1830s and 1840s, street names in what would become the Washington Square neighborhood were in transition.

Sixth Street was named Waverly Place in 1833 in honor of Sir Walter Scott and his novel *Waverley* [sic]. The spelling error remains on street signs to this day.

Art Place, originally Sand Hill, became Astor Place for John Jacob Astor.

Eighth Street was Clinton Place, in honor of the Clintons—George, first governor of the state of New York, and his nephew, DeWitt, mayor of the city of New York.

Ninth Street from Fifth Avenue to Broadway was Randall Lane and Tenth Street between Fifth Avenue and Broadway was Brevoort Lane, each named for the farms that preceded the streets.

University Place was Wooster Street for David Wooster, a Revolutionary War hero. Like Wooster, MacDougal (another misspelling—McDougal is correct), Sullivan, Thompson, Greene, and Mercer were named after Revolutionary War generals. For a time in 1828, Wooster between Eighth and Fourteenth Streets was Jackson Place for President Andrew Jackson.

THE
SAILORS' SNUG HARBOR

Thomas Randall: Privateer, Patriot, Entrepreneur

The story of The Sailors' Snug Harbor—America's oldest secular philanthropic foundation—begins with the arrival in New York in the 1740s of a young and obscure seaman from Scotland named Thomas Randall.[1] He was just in time to take part in King George's War, one of the intermittent armed struggles that pitted Great Britain against France on a worldwide battlefield for the better part of a century. By the time the shooting came to a temporary

A view of New York Bay and Harbor from Staten Island early in the Nineteenth Century.

halt in 1748, Randall's exploits as a privateer had caught the attention of New York's mariners and merchants. He had first come to public notice when the *New York Post-Boy* described the capture of a French prize by Randall's *Dolphin* and the *Prince Frederick* under a Captain Marshall of Providence. With a bit of hometown puffery, the editor made slighting remarks about Marshall's role in the seizure. Randall promptly rushed to the Rhode Islander's defense and demanded that the editor issue a public apology. Randall later commanded the *Fox*, a sloop with 14 guns and a crew of 100. The ship counted among its prizes the French navy's *Amazone*—a notable triumph because privateers normally avoided heavily armed warships.

With peace, Randall devoted himself to his family and to mercantile interests. Sometime during the war he had married Gertrude Crooke, and they eventually had three sons and a daughter. He developed a shipping trade, sending notions and other items to New Orleans and the West Indies in exchange for sugar, molasses, and rum.

In 1756, the French and English were at it once again in what is known abroad as the Seven Years War and to Americans as the French and Indian War. By the time peace returned in 1763, Thomas Randall was America's best known privateer.

The Business of Privateering

The terms *privateer* and *pirate* or *licensed pirate* are often used interchangeably in histories of this period. Around 1700, when William Kidd was a notable New Yorker, the relationship between these occupations had been a close one, but piracy was suppressed by the Crown early in the century and privateering was formalized as a speculative wartime business venture. The government showed no tolerance for infractions of its prize laws. A letter of marque, or privateering commission, had to be signed both by the provincial governor and a judge of the vice admiralty. As Stuyvesant Fish points out in *The New York Privateers: 1756-1763*, "The list of privateers might well be called the 'Social Register.' Among their number were two signers of the Declaration of Independence and seventeen members of the Vestry of Trinity Church which testifies to the fact that this pursuit was considered a highly honorable one." Fish adds, "In those days wealthy fathers bought privateering vessels for their sons rather than the stock exchange seats they get today." James G. Lydon writes in *Pirates, Privateers, and Profits*, "Privateers cannot be dismissed as either rascals or pirates even if they helped their country by helping themselves." James Grant Wilson notes in his history of New York that the spoils brought home by privateers were the foundation of many a New York fortune.[2]

At the opening of this final phase of the long war, New York stood fourth in import-export tonnage among American ports, trailing behind Philadelphia, Boston, and Charleston. But it ranked first in the matter of colonial privateering. Nearly 200 armed merchant ships, sanctioned by the Crown and underwritten by businessmen who shared in the booty, sailed from New York before the final French defeat.

The first captured French vessel brought into New York harbor in 1756 was escorted by Thomas Randall. Four months later, the *New York Mercury* reported that Captain Randall "had captured the finest French privateer in the West Indies." A seven-month sweep through the West Indies aboard the 20-gun sloop *Goldfinch* was the most dangerous and profitable of Randall's wartime ventures. In December 1756, Captain Randall wrote to the owners, merchants John Aspinwall and John Kortright, that he had captured two French vessels and salvaged the cargo of another "cast away upon the island of Mayaguina" in the Bahamas. On December 9, "in the Bite of Leoganne [Haiti]" he destroyed a French privateer. About 12 hours later, he met the *Charming Sally*, a sloop captained by Richard Harris and owned by John Jauncey and John Lawrence, wealthy New Yorkers. A week later *Goldfinch* and *Charming Sally* intercepted a French privateer and her English prize. Following a four-hour battle, in which the *Goldfinch* took 30 hits, the French struck their colors. Neither Yankee vessel lost a man, while the French suffered 5 dead and 11 wounded.

In his letter to the owners of the *Goldfinch*, Randall apologized for not "adorning your harbor with rich ships." "Yet," he added, "we have the satisfaction of knowing that we serve our country by taking the Enemy Ships of War, this being the 4th French Privateer we have been concern'd in reducing during this Cruize." Before signing off, he said he was "now going after some Ships we have intelligence are ready to sail."[3]

The following Letter is from on board Capt. Randle, dated at Hineago, December 24th, 1756, just before he sent the Prize away.

"....On the 9th Instant, cruizing in the Bite of Leogann, we met a French Sloop of 10 Guns, bound from St. Marck, to Porto Prince, in order to be commissioned for a Privateer, but soon stopped her Course, took her Guns, and every Thing of Value out, and she being very old and leaky, sunk her. About 12 Hours after we met Capt. Richard Harris, in a Privateer Sloop from New-York, whom we have been with ever since. On the 10th, being off Cape St. Nicholas, we saw two Sail, one of which proved to be the Privateer we now send you, and her Prize, being the Sloop Delight, Daniel Seymour, Master, from New-York, bound to Jamaica, whom she had taken about 36 Hours before. We first retook Capt. Seymour, and by that Time our Consort, Capt. Harris, came up, and began the Engagement with us; we first receiving thirty-odd Shot from the Privateer: And after engaging four Hours and a Half, she struck to us, having 5 Men killed, and 11 wounded. Our Consort and our-

Excerpt from a report to the shipowners by Thomas Randall, captain of their 20-gun privateer Goldfinch

When the *Goldfinch* returned to New York, it escorted eight prizes valued at nearly £10,000 sterling. Soon after, Randall was listed as an owner along with Aspinwall and Kortright. The threesome were also partners in the *DeLancey*, which was being fitted out for another Randall voyage. Captain Randall owned or partially owned three other privateers including the *Charming Sally*. In the usual letter of marque, owners and captains each received a 5 percent share of the prize. Thus, in his double role, Randall must have been rewarded handsomely.

NEW-YORK AIR FURNACE.

PETER T. CURTENIUS, and Co.

Advertisement for New-York Air Furnace. Thomas Randall was one of four partners who built the furnace in 1767 to manufacture cast-iron products. It was located on the North River shore "near Mr. Atlee's brewery."

One of Randall's Caribbean adventures was revealed in 1828, some 70 years after it happened, in a letter from the U.S. Consul in Paris, I. Cox Barnet, to Captain John Whetten, president of the Sailors' Snug Harbor Board of Trustees. The letter, which involved evidence in a lawsuit against the trustees, contained an interesting aside from Barnet. He recalled that the life of young Thomas Randall was saved "very providentially from a party of banditti, near Nassau, New Providence, by my maternal grandfather, Colonel James Stowe, who resided at the latter place."[4]

Peace and Prosperity

Peace, and victory for England, found the doughty warrior, at age 32, wealthy, ambitious, and one of the important men in the city of New York. Captain Randall built a house in Whitehall at the corner of Pearl Street on the southern tip of Manhattan and began to invest in real estate. Eventually, he was the owner of nearly a dozen lots and houses in the heart of town; a 23-acre farm in Chatham, New Jersey; and Minto, the 21-acre Manhattan farm that was the future home of Sailors' Snug Harbor. In addition, he bought land along the Pee Dee River in South Carolina where he traded extensively.

In 1767, he joined three other entrepreneurs to build on the

Hudson shore an air furnace for iron casting. It turned out pots, stoves, chafing dishes, forge hammers, plow plates, and other useful products that were advertised as "equal to any imported from England, Scotland, Ireland, or even Holland."[5] Many of these articles were likely to have found their way into the holds of his trading ships, still the principal Randall enterprise.

Eve of Revolution

England's capture of Canada and Guadeloupe—richest of the Caribbean sugar islands—along with victories in India, Africa, and Europe, brought the worldwide conflict between Britain, France, and their allies to an end in 1760. Before a treaty was signed in Paris in 1763, however, Britain had to make the type of decision that has spawned a popular divertissement on today's college campuses—alternate history or "what if" history. (A current example is Peter G. Tsouras's *Gettysburg: An Alternate History,* "answering every Civil War buff's question, 'What If?'") For England, the "what if" was Canada or Guadeloupe, lands that were prized equally by most influential Englishmen. Canada was huge but barren; Voltaire observed that it was "only a few acres of snow." Guadeloupe was an agricultural gold mine, producing sugar, rum, coffee, and tobacco. Even William Pitt, creator of Great Britain's powerful fleet and armies, was of two minds about the issue. It is reported that he exclaimed, "Some are for keeping Canada, some Guadeloupe: who will tell me which I shall be hanged for not keeping." The pro-Canada party finally prevailed, but at a disconcerting cost. As Winston Churchill noted almost two centuries later, "The extinction of the French menace [in North America] would lead to the final secession of the English colonies from the British Empire."[6]

Seventy years of war had saddled Britain with an enormous public debt that the mother country felt should be shared in part by the American colonies. Parliament, abandoning what Edmund Burke called a policy of "salutary neglect," and a newly crowned George III embarked on a series of ill-advised measures designed to turn the clock back on what had become an irresistible move toward home rule. The Stamp Act, requiring duties on most printed matters, was the first direct tax imposed on the colonies. This legislation, along with Parliament's strict enforcement of the navigation and trade acts, led to colonial boycotts of goods from Britain.

A letter to Parliament from the merchants of New York—written by

William Livingston, the city's most literate radical—explained the adverse effects of the new duties and rigorous enforcement of the trade laws. "Imports from England in 1763 exceeded New York's exports to Great Britain by $468,217. To survive, New York has to be free to trade itself out of debt by sending flour and lumber to the French and Spanish Indies in return for sugar, molasses, and hard currency. . . .This wealth ultimately ends up in Britain." The letter was ignored.⁷

In October 1765, representatives of nine colonies came to New York's city hall on Wall Street to convene the Stamp Act Congress, which protested against taxation without representation. Many historians regard that meeting as the opening move toward the American Revolution. All five of the New York delegates were colleagues of Thomas Randall, now one of the most influential of the city's merchant captains. He was among the 24 founders of the chamber of commerce in 1768. A year later, 32 of the city's leading mariners and merchants agreed to form a society that would care for distressed shipmasters and their widows and orphans. Randall headed the committee that drew up the articles that led to a royal charter for The Marine Society of the City of New York in April 1770. He was elected as the second president of the society in January 1774 and served until the British occupied New York in September 1776.

These were busy and difficult days for Randall. His eldest son, Thomas Jr., who had joined him as a founder of The Marine Society, was killed in an accident at sea in 1772. As reported in the *New York Gazette and Weekly Mercury*: "Last Wednesday Capt. Thomas Randle Jun., of this port, inward bound from the West Indies, a few miles from Sandy Hook, was knocked overboard with the Boom and drowned. He was a promising youth, and his death is greatly lamented by all his acquaintances."

When the Boston Tea Party provoked Parliament to enact the Coercive Acts in 1774, which blockaded the port of Boston and empowered royal governors to quarter troops in private homes, New York was among the first colonies to form a committee of patriots to coordinate its actions with the other colonies, to instruct delegates to the First Continental Congress in Philadelphia, to identify loyalists, and to boycott English goods.

On the committee, Randall was an ally of Alexander McDougal, Isaac Sears, and John Lamb, who were principal founders of the Sons of Liberty in New York (a secret society that harried royal officials

throughout the decade leading up to the Revolution). Like Randall, McDougal and Sears had been privateers in the French and Indian War who became successful merchants. McDougal, commander of West Point after Benedict Arnold's treason, was jailed for a time in 1771 for writing a pamphlet entitled "To the Betrayed Inhabitants of the City and Colony of New York." He would later serve as the first president of Alexander Hamilton's Bank of New York. Lamb, commander of a renowned artillery company during the French and Indian War, was accused by Randall's loyalist successor as president of The Marine Society of making off with the organization's official seal. Perhaps the plaque ended up on Randall's wall, but the records do not say what happened to it. The boycott of English goods was enforced in New York by an inspection committee that patrolled the waterfront. Randall was one of the inspectors.

The year 1774 was also the year in which Stephen Girard sailed into Randall's life. At age 23 and already a shipmaster, Girard had embarked from Bordeaux, his home port, for Port-au-Prince with a cargo bought on credit. Business was bad, so Girard sold the ship and the cargo at a loss. With the cash he chartered a brig, loaded it with sugar and coffee, and sailed to New York. There, he was able to pay off

The Great Fire of 1776. This French print by Francois Xavier Haberman is said to be based on eye-witness accounts "du feu terrible a Nouvelle Yorck" in September 1776.

his creditors and he met Captain Randall, who was impressed with the young man from France. Randall hired Girard as first mate for his *L'Amiable Louise* and soon promoted him to captain and junior partner. In the spring of 1776, Girard took cargo to Hispaniola on *La Jeune Babe*. Before the *Babe* could return to her home port, the colonists had proclaimed the Declaration of Independence and Britain had blockaded New York. Girard slipped up the Delaware River to Philadelphia. Meanwhile, Captain Randall and his son Robert Richard, in business as Thomas Randall & Son, shifted their operations from occupied New York to Elizabeth Town, New Jersey, not far from Randall's farm in Chatham. On a visit to Philadelphia, Randall, Girard, and Isaac Hazelhurst formed a joint, three-vessel trading company that they had to abandon in early 1777 because of the blockade. Girard and Randall corresponded frequently about business and family matters. A postscript on one of Randall's letters asks Girard to write in English "as my daughter is a very bad translator."

By the end of the war, the entrepreneurial partners had gone their separate ways. Girard was to develop a worldwide trading fleet that laid the foundation of his great wealth. After the federal government declined to extend the charter of the first Bank of the United States in 1811, he bought its assets, including the Philadelphia headquarters, and established the Bank of Stephen Girard. When the government attempted to finance the War of 1812 with $16 million in bonds, the sale went poorly until Girard and John Jacob Astor arranged to take a $10 million share.[8] When Girard died on December 26, 1831, he bequeathed most of his fortune to the city of Philadelphia for the founding of Girard College to educate poor, white, orphan boys.

Exile and Restoration

In Elizabeth Town, the Randalls had spent much of their time fitting out privateers commissioned by the Continental Congress. During this period, Robert Richard Randall may have shipped out as a privateer. That is conjecture, but one of the few facts that we can verify about him can lead to such a supposition. Early in 1776, when the provincial legislature began raising several battalions, young Randall petitioned for a company commission "tho' totally unacquainted with" military ways. He was turned down. Usually, wealthy young volunteers, however ignorant of the arts of war, were welcomed into the service. It has been suggested that the authorities thought Robert Richard would be of more use to the revolutionary cause by going to sea. Stuyvesant Fish wrote that Thomas Randall had a "bad-tempered son to whom he left his fortune. This son, Robert Richard Randall, followed in his father's footsteps. He also privateered and saved his money." Unfortunately, Fish did not record the source of his information.

The Randalls were back in New York almost as soon as the last of the Redcoats withdrew from the city in November 1783, more than two years after Cornwallis's surrender at Yorktown. The business, now known as Randall, Son and Stewart, Merchants, selling dry goods and ironware, was reestablished at 10 Hanover Square. Captain Randall's new partner, Alexander Stewart, was a founding member of The Marine Society. Randall's house and shop had been spared in the fire that destroyed as much as a sixth of New York on September 21, 1776, shortly after the British occupied the city. Flames consumed all but a few buildings on the west side of Broadway, including Trinity Church. Was the city torched, as General Nathaniel Greene advised, or did the fire start accidentally in a wooden tavern near Whitehall Slip and spread before gale-force winds? It is still a matter of debate among historians.[9]

When General George Washington came to the liberated city to bid farewell to his officers at Fraunces Tavern, he was greeted by a committee of 13 citizens who had "returned from exile." The first name on the list of exiles was Thomas Randall. Randall, a member of the vestry at Trinity Church, was a somewhat unusual "exile." Anglicans in New York, especially clergy, were usually loyalists; Presbyterians, who were dissenters by tradition, were generally patriots. When the British took over the city, Pastor John Rogers and his congregation at the First Presbyterian Church on Wall Street scattered. During the seven-year occupation, the Redcoats used their church as a barracks and later as a stable.

Following the long occupation, both the chamber of commerce and The Marine Society were in disarray. Randall figured importantly in their revitalization. He was also a member of the first board of aldermen to serve

The Tontine Coffee House, precursor of the New York Stock Exchange, stood on the northwest corner of Wall and Water Streets. The Randalls, father and sons, were members.

under the American flag, a founding director of Alexander Hamilton's Bank of New York, and a shareholder in the Tontine Coffee House, a precursor of the New York Stock Exchange.

A Randall or Two, Too Many

Busy man that he was, Randall was never—as reported—American vice consul in Canton, China. A Thomas Randall and his friend, Samuel Shaw, sailed in February 1784 from New York to Canton as supercargoes—the owners' business agents—on the *Empress of China*, the epic voyage that originated Yankee-Chinese trade. This Randall and Shaw were Boston merchants who had served together in a Massachusetts artillery unit during the Revolution. Shaw was a friend of John Jay, then secretary of foreign affairs for the Continental Congress. As the first American businessman to visit China, Shaw was appointed consul. As late as the 1930s, the U.S. State Department still confused the Thomas Randalls, as can be seen in its response to an inquiry about whether the New York Randall had ever held a governmental position. The State Department answered, yes, Thomas Randall had been vice consul in Canton. (The letter is in the Sailors' Snug Harbor archives at Fort Schulyer in the Bronx.)[10]

A more troubling mix-up in names involved a Thomas Randall who was active in the slave trade. An undated clipping from an unnamed newspaper is part of *Annals and Occurrences of New York City and State in the Olden Time,* a potpourri of information, gossip, and news reports put together in 1846 by John F. Watson. The following report appears on page 269: "A parcel of fine young slaves just imported in the schooner *Catherine* from the coast of Africa are for sale at Moore's wharf by Thomas Randall and J. Alexander." Almost certainly this is still another Thomas Randall. Although *Catherine*, the name of the slave ship, was also the name of Thomas Randall's only daughter, this schooner was built in New Jersey in the 1730s, long before Randall arrived in New York. *Catherine*, under Captain John Lewis, fell to a slave insurrection in 1761.[11]

In 1932, the Carnegie Institution published Elizabeth Donnan's four-volume *Documents Illustrative of the History of the Slave Trade to America*. Its exhaustive gleaning of custom house entries, naval office listings, and news clippings lists the names, masters, and owners of ships and the size of their slave cargoes. Thomas Randall is named as captain of a sloop carrying slaves that arrived in the port of New

York on July 14, 1721, just about two years before our Thomas was born in Scotland. This Thomas is most likely an Englishman from the port of Weymouth who was frequently in trouble with the police because of smuggling. Local authorities reported that he delivered a cargo of slaves to Barbados in 1709.[12] Donnan's data, comprehensive as they are, show gaps because old records have a way of vanishing.

The research of James G. Lydon, referred to previously for his *Pirates, Privateers, and Profits*, is as authoritative as one can get on the subject of Thomas Randall. In a 1978 discussion about slavery in New York in the William and Mary Quarterly, Lydon reported that 100 merchants and captains shared ownership in slave ships including many prominent citizens and "several successful privateer captains in King George's War." The name Thomas Randall does not appear on Lydon's list of nearly 50 important New Yorkers who speculated in African trading.

The only names reported in the first U.S. Census in 1790 are those identified as heads of households. Living with Thomas Randall in his lower-Manhattan home were one "free white male over 16" (presumably Paul, the youngest son) and two "free white females" (presumably Randall's wife and daughter). The census reported no slaves living in Randall's household, although more than 20 percent of his neighbors listed one or more slaves as part of their household.

The Grand Convention

By 1787, the eleventh anniversary of independence, most Americans had come to realize that something better than the Articles of Confederation was needed to keep the young republic from splintering into a league of petty sovereignties. Delegates from all the states but Rhode Island convened in Philadelphia from May 25 to September 17 to hammer out what would be a completely new constitution for the United States, to take effect when ratified by nine states.

With New Hampshire's ratification in June 1788, the bitterly divided state of New York had to sign on or withdraw from the Union. The Federalists, advocating strong national government, were led in New York by Alexander Hamilton and John Jay. The anti-Federalists, who equated liberty with localism, followed the banner of Governor George Clinton and a majority of upstate legislators. Three days before the state convention at Poughkeepsie that would vote on the question of adoption, the Federalists staged a huge parade on Broadway in support of ratification. The parade featured a full-rigged, 32-gun miniature frigate named the "Alexander Hamilton," which was drawn by 10 horses and staffed by a uniformed crew of 30. The parade ended at the Bayard farm near the Bowery where an open-air dinner was served to 5,000 celebrants representing 60 trades and professions. Even more important to the Federalist cause than that show of strength may have been a threat made by Hamilton. He warned that if the delegates at Poughkeepsie failed to ratify, New York City and its environs would secede from New York State, form a state of its own, and ratify the compact. "And where," Hamilton asked, "will the Empire State be without its crown jewel?"[13] On July 26, 1788, New York voted to ratify the new constitution by a mere 30 to 27.

One of the last acts of the expiring Continental Congress was to select New York City as the nation's new capital.

Randall's Great Barge

On April 6, 1789, electors chosen by their state legislators gathered at Federal Hall on Wall Street to elect George Washington as president and John Adams as vice president of the United States. Washington began a triumphal procession from Mount Vernon on April 16, arriving at Elizabeth Town, New Jersey, on April 23 for the journey's final leg via a magnificent 45-foot barge to Murray's festooned wharf at the foot of Wall Street on the East River. The barge, conceived in the mind of Thomas Randall, was transported by 13 oarsmen dressed in white with Randall at the tiller. Following a week of festive ceremony, Washington stepped onto the balcony of Federal Hall on April 30 to take the oath of this revolutionary new office. When Congress adjourned in August, after voting to move the U.S. capital to Philadelphia, Washington wrote a friendly note to Randall. The president returned the elegant barge, for which he would have no further use, but he told Captain Randall and its other owners that he had accepted their beautiful present "as a pledge of that real urbanity, which I am happy in declaring I have experienced on every occasion during my residence among them."[14]

Governor George Clinton appointed Captain Randall to his final civic post, Master Warden of the Port of New York and the lighthouse at Sandy Hook. Randall resigned on September 29, 1794, explaining that his "advanced age and the active duties of the office render it inconvenient for . . . [him] to attend any longer to it." The old captain lived on for another three years, dying at age 74 on October 27, 1797. He is buried in the family vault in the Trinity Church graveyard.

His will directed the executors to sell the Chatham farm and some downtown lots, to pay his widow £800 per year, and to turn the house at Whitehall over to his widow and unmarried daughter Catherine. Each of the children—Robert Richard, Paul, and Catherine—received three rent-paying properties in the city. Robert Richard also inherited the Minto farm, where he had been living since 1790. Because, in the words of the will, "Robert Richard will receive a larger proportion than by right he ought to receive," he was instructed to pay £2,000 each to his brother and sister. All three children were named executors but, as time would tell, Catherine's appointment had unusual significance.

The Randall Farm

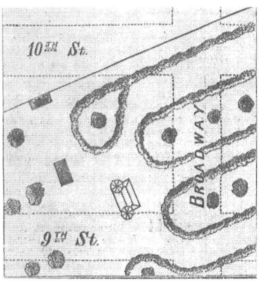

The farmland that was to become the Sailors' Snug Harbor in the nineteenth century was among the first properties cultivated by colonists in Manhattan.[15] Early on, it consisted of two grants from the Dutch West India Company, one to Cosyn Gerritsen, the other to Pieter Stoutenburgh. By 1639 Gerritsen had a house and garden on five acres of land that bordered to the south on "a certain swamp," surely part of the future Washington Square Park. Within four years, company documents mentioned "Cosyn Gerritsen's wagon way," running west from what was to become the Bowery road toward Minetta Creek. This later became Sand Hill Road, and still later the beginning section of Greenwich Avenue. The Sand Hills were a low range extending in a semicircular course from the Bowery toward the Hudson River.

Sketch of Minto as shown in Valentine's Manual.

Adrian van Schaick, long-time proprietor of the Plow and Harrow Tavern "at the two-mile stone," bought the Gerritsen farm in 1679 and expanded it to 15 acres. After his death in 1700, his widow ran the tavern, which became well known as "Rebecca's House." In 1722, the land was sold for £250 to Richard Pero, "Mariner." Pero was apparently lost at sea during a voyage to Jamaica in 1736. His widow, Giddy, and the Pero children sold the property for £308 in 1767 to Andrew Elliot, crown collector of the port of New York and the man who unified the grant lands into the more than 21-acre farm that the Randalls acquired in 1790.

Pieter Stoutenburgh's eight-acre grant, dated April 7, 1664, was immediately to the north of the Gerritsen farm and just west of, and formerly a part of, Governor Peter Stuyvesant's large estate. Around 1700, the date is uncertain, this tract came into possession of Captain Giles Shelley, who in 1699 was with Captain William Kidd in Madagascar, principal lair of Indian Ocean pirates. Rather than sail directly into the harbor on his return to New York, Shelley made landfall in New Jersey. There, his merchant partners, including a member of the eminent De Lancey family, unloaded the most valuable parts of his cargo of 15,000 gold and silver coins, ivory, opium, exotic textiles, and slaves. Questioned by the authorities, Shelley confessed only to importing slaves, which was no offense at all. Kidd returned a few weeks later, first burying his treasures on Gardner's Island and at Orient Point, where Long Island's Peconic Bay meets the Atlantic Ocean. Partly on Shelley's word that his compere really was a pirate, Kidd was arrested, shipped to England in irons, and hanged on May 23, 1701. Shelley, in 1710, willed his land to Edward Antill "whom I have adopted and bread [sic] up, having no children of my own." Whitehead Hicks, an attorney who was mayor of New York for the 10 years preceding the American Revolution, received the property from Antill in 1754, perhaps in a foreclosure. Hicks never lived on the farm, which was sold in 1766 by Daniel Horsmanden for £850 to Andrew Elliot. Horsmanden played the principal role in New York's more murderous version of the Salem witch trials. As a justice of the provincial supreme court, he presided over a series of conspiracy trials in 1741 that led to the execution of 31 black and 4 white "plotters," even though much of the evidence was questionable. In 1744, Horsmanden published a 400-page defense of the trials based on his own notes, those of two fellow judges, and the lawyers on the various cases.

Portions of both Dutch grants had been owned by slaves freed by the West India Company in the 1640s, shortly after a treaty with the Algonquin Indians had ended a war that destroyed all but a few farms in the shadow of Fort Amsterdam. The slaves were freed, said the Dutch, for long and faithful service. Recent studies suggest that there was at least as much expediency as altruism in this act of manumission.[16] The Negro lots, as they were known, ran along the west side of what was to become Broadway, below Union Square, through Astor

Place to Prince Street. Thus, the land formed a buffer zone against the Indians who remained in northern Manhattan.

Andrew Elliot, appointed collector of the port of New York in 1774 and lieutenant governor of New York in 1780, came from a distinguished family of Scots.[17] His new country estate was named Minto after an uncle, the Earl of Minto. He built a handsome, brick, octagon-shaped mansion on a hill fronting Bowery Road, just above what is now Ninth Street. Elliot was acting governor for a time, sitting in for General William Tryon, who led a strong force of Loyalists along the Hudson and in southern Connecticut. Tryon, who had been governor of colonial North Carolina, was transferred to New York shortly before the outbreak of the Revolution. Less than three weeks before the British evacuation of New York on November 25, 1783, Elliot sold his estate for £2,800 to Abel James and returned to England with his family. Elliott had been one of the royal officials most admired by the colonists. As collector of customs, he had warned the governor in the days before the war that "certain groups of Loyalists were notorious for engaging in the ugliest kinds of violence." "War would be counterproductive," he added, "and would simply fill British prisons with victims of private revenge." When a shortage of specie threatened trade, Elliott accepted promissory notes. This helped make him popular with businessmen and shipmasters alike, because the custom house was not run "with vigor and cruelty" as was common in other ports. Both contingencies came to his support when he was challenged by the Sons of Liberty in December 1774. After customs officials seized a smuggled shipment of arms and powder, Isaac Sears, leader of the patriots, threatened "to set the mob" on Elliott unless he returned the confiscated weaponry. Some 300 ship captains and seamen plus scores of merchants, learning of the danger, assembled before the custom house in a show of support for Elliott. Sears backed off. In 1778, Elliott became superintendent-general of police as well as collector. His refusal to bend the laws in favor of the military upset some of his fellow Englishmen.

In March 1785, James sold Minto for £4,000 to John Jay, Isaac Roosevelt, and Alexander Hamilton. Sometime in 1786 or shortly thereafter, the deed belonged to Frederick Charles Hans Bruno Poelnitz, who called himself Baron. The baron, a horticulturist, turned the land into a showplace by planting a remarkable variety of fruit trees and flowering shrubs. Among his visitors in the spring of 1789 was the new nation's most influential farmer, President George Washington.

Robert Richard Randall: Gentleman Farmer

In a deed dated June 15, 1790, the baron conveyed his premises in the city's new seventh ward to Robert Richard Randall for £5,000 or $12,500. Robert most likely signed the deed as his father's agent. Although Minto was the younger Randall's home, the father's will leaves no doubt that he, Thomas, owned it. The elder Randall continued to live at Whitehall and on the Chatham farm.

Robert Richard, born about 1750, seems to have retired from his father's firm to live the country life of a gentleman bachelor in what was a pleasant and well-to-do rural community two miles north of the city.[18] His nearest neighbor was Henry Brevoort—the fifth of that name in a family that had farmed the acres between Tenth and Sixteenth Streets for nearly 150 years. Brevoort, who lived in a house on the site now occupied by Grace Church, left his mark on Manhattan geography by proving that one can fight city hall. Because Brevoort refused to let the city commissioners cut through his land to implement their 1811 street grid plan for Manhattan, Broadway bends at Tenth Street, and Eleventh Street, abruptly interrupted on the west side of Broadway, starts again at the Bowery on the east side of Brevoort's property. He won his fight despite two ordinances ordering him to give way.[19]

Among other neighbors who shared conversation and rum punches were the Stuyvesants, the Wilmerdings, and the Sperrys, whose farm touched Randall's land on the south. Jacob Sperry, a Swiss physician, laid out extensive gardens on his 28 acres that extended from the future Astor Place to Fourth Street. He sold the land in 1804 for $45,000 to John Jacob Astor, a cousin by marriage of Henry Brevoort. Astor immediately leased the land to a French showman, Joseph Delacroix, who converted the property into a maze of gravel walks, flower beds, arbors, fountains, refreshment booths, and an open-air musical theater. Fireworks and balloon ascensions added zest to Delacroix's Vauxhall Gardens. When the lease expired in 1825, Astor cut Lafayette Place through the gardens, reducing the property in size by half. The choice residential lots Astor sold brought him multiples of the $45,000 he originally paid for the property. At midcentury, the still popular gardens became the site of the Astor Library.

Robert's sister Catherine, soon to marry James Brewerton, had written to her brother shortly after their father's death that she wished to cooperate as an executor of the will "in the most harmonious manner."

"But," she added, "not understanding business, I have—according to the advice of our Father while alive—engaged the legal assistance of General Hamilton, who will, on my part confer with you as occasion may require."

Brother Paul had come upon hard times. Unable to pay his business bills, he fled to France rather than face debtor's prison, a fearsome threat. At the very time that Paul was becoming a bankrupt, the failed speculations of Robert Morris landed this signer of the Declaration of Independence and "financier of the American Revolution" in prison for three years. Morris died in poverty and obscurity.

Robert received an embittered letter from Paul, dated May 1, 1800. "My sufferings, loss in property, in liberty, languishing in irons and in prisons, a victim of the want of justice everywhere—to the imbecility of our own government and to the rapacity and infamous disposition of others, condemned to starve in this great capital of the world, without a friend to succor me here—absolutely abandoned by my family and friends at home—can anyone judge of the desperation of my feelings." Paul never returned to the United States and died in Paris in 1820.

The Randall Will

Less than four years after his father's death, Robert Richard Randall died on June 5, 1801. Four days earlier his remarkable will had been constructed.[20]

First, a few minor bequests. He left his gold sleeve buttons and an annuity of £40 per year to his housekeeper Betsey Hart; his gold watch and the sum of £40 to his overseer Adam Shields; and his shoe and knee buckles and the sum of £20 to his friend Gawn Irwin.

Then came a series of bold and significant imperatives bequeathing the remainder of the estate to a rather astounding array of public, civic, and religious leaders in New York who were instructed to build upon his farm "an asylum, or Marine Hospital, to be called 'The Sailors' Snug Harbor,' for the purpose of maintaining and supporting aged, decrepit and worn-out sailors as soon as . . . the proceeds of said estate will support fifty of the said sailors, and upwards." The institution was to be "perpetual" and governed "forever" by those holding the offices of chancellor of the state, mayor and recorder of the city, president of the chamber of commerce, president and vice president of The Marine Society, and senior ministers of the Episcopal and Presbyterian churches. All courts of law and equity were called upon "to have the said estate appropriated to the above uses" and in no case to construe it so that "my relations or any other persons should heir, possess or enjoy my property except in the manner and for the uses herein-above specified." Finally, he decreed that the persons listed as "governors" should be executors of the estate.

The estate was relatively modest, even though it was likely that Minto had increased in value since the Randalls had acquired it 11 years earlier for $12,500. The total estate, which also included four lots in the first ward of the city and some bank stock, was worth about $15,000. In the language of the will, there was a clear expectation that the value of the estate would increase considerably.

That was only one of Randall's optimistic assumptions. In addition, he expected that eight of the most important men in the city would accept for themselves, and their successors, the responsibilities laid upon them to care for a class of persons whose standing in the society of the day was not very high. Many years later, A. Barton Hepburn, a financier and president of the chamber of commerce, remarked: "Just ponder for a moment on how ridiculous it is that a man one hundred and ten years ago, could point out this man as the person who must devote ten thousand dollars worth of his time each year acting as a trustee of Mr. Randall's estate. Why, I wouldn't do the work that, as a trustee I am compelled to do, for twenty-five thousand dollars a year. But I do not have the right, by the terms of Mr. Randall's will to decline to act. It is strange though, when you come to think of it, that this thing can be."

One troublesome feature of the will was Randall's treatment of kith and kin. The will specifically disowned his relations, even though his brother Paul was in humiliating financial straits. He left nothing to his sister Catherine. The will did provide legacies for Paul's legitimate children, if any. Years later, as part of a lawsuit brought by reputed Randall heirs, the American consul in Paris reported that Paul had died without issue.

Now, the enigma about the will. Whoever wrote or inspired it was a person of courage and foresight. Sailors' Snug Harbor tradition gives the credit to Alexander Hamilton, an old family friend who had drawn Thomas Randall's will, and to his assistant, Daniel D. Tomkins, who would become fifth governor of New York and sixth vice president of the United States. Hamilton, the nation's first secretary of the treasury, was practicing law in New York in 1801 and might well have had dealings with Robert Richard while representing Catherine in her executor duties. The problem with this scenario is that the only mention of the younger Randall's will in *The Papers of Alexander Hamilton* appears as a lengthy editor's note in volume 25: "H [Hamilton] is credited with having drawn up a will which subsequently attracted considerable attention. . . . Randall, who was a privateer during the American Revolution, had an enduring interest in the welfare of sailors." The editor's note continues with a report about another legal matter involving Hamilton—whether the newly built St. Mark's in the Bowery Episcopal Church should be a chapel within the parish of Trinity Church, as originally intended, or independent. An opinion attributed to Hamilton and an associate served as the basis for the establishment of a separate St. Mark's. "Although H's part in drawing up the Randall will and his opinion concerning St. Mark's church have both received considerable publicity," the editor adds, "the original of neither document has been found."

The Law Practice of Alexander Hamilton is a five-volume documentary reconstruction of Hamilton's legal work. Its preface contains the following caveat: "Profuse as are the materials relating to his large and varied practice . . . they are [often] too fragmentary to further our inquiry."

Proof is lacking but, according to legend, Robert Richard had asked Hamilton about the best way to dispose of his estate. Hamilton is said to have replied, "It came from the sea, let it go back to the sea." Isaac Bell, a wealthy merchant who probably knew the younger Randall and Hamilton through his membership in The Marine Society, regaled associates with this story in the early 1800s.

Others have argued that the idea of a home for seamen could have originated in the mind of the senior Randall and that it was his plan that was given reality in Robert Richard's will. Still others, noting the great charitable work of Stephen Girard, see the wealthy Philadelphian as Randall's inspiration—even though Girard's will was written a quarter of a century after that of Robert Richard.

That the younger Randall might well have conceived the plan on his own was unacceptable to many people, even those connected with the Harbor. By the 1870s, Harbor Governor Thomas Melville expressed doubts that Robert Richard had ever been a sea captain. An article in *Century* magazine in 1884 claimed that Randall's will resulted from his lawyers' prompting rather than from his own personal interest in the welfare of old sailors. How anyone could know such things decades later is puzzling because Robert Richard left few tracks during his life-time. Among the few certainties is that those who knew him called him "Captain."

Through his membership in The Marine Society, young Randall was familiar with the welfare needs of ill-starred merchant captains and their families. It is likely that he knew about England's famed Royal Hospital at Greenwich, founded a century earlier to care for aged veterans of the British navy. Randall's Sailors' Snug Harbor was perceived as something grander than either of its predecessors, welcoming all seamen regardless of rank, nationality, religion, or race. It has, to date, provided a final haven for more than 14,000 sailors when their days at sea were finished.

Notes

1. The Harbor's claim to be America's oldest secular philanthropy is based on more than tradition. What was once the Central Hanover Bank and Trust Company before it vanished in a sea of mergers maintained a library of unpublished manuscripts written by its officers about the most important foundations. (See "Report of the Princeton Conference on the History of Philanthropy in the United States; Russell Sage Foundation," 1956.) A copy of the bank's 17-page report on the Harbor in 1937 is available at Fort Schuyler. Author John Clapp identified the Harbor as "the oldest" American foundation. Amos G. Warner in *American Charities*, the standard historical work about foundations, notes that what could be called philanthropy during the colonial period and the early nineteenth century was church-related.

2. See James G. Lydon, *Pirates, Privateers, and Profits* for privateering as a business. See also James Grant Wilson, *The Memorial History of the City of New York.*

3. A copy of Randall's letter to the owners of the *Goldfinch* is in the Library of Congress. A photocopy of it belongs to Mel Hardin, curator of the Sailors' Snug Harbor art collection.

4. The letter from Consul Barnet in Paris is quoted in Don Seitz's history of the Harbor, p. 174.

5. An engraving of the air furnace and the advertisement that appears with it is available in the New-York Historical Society. Also see John A. Kouwenhoven, *The Columbia Historical Portrait of New York*, p. 100.

6. Pitt's quote is reported in Theodore Draper's *A Struggle for Power* (p. 16), a scholarly and original study of the events and voices that led to the American Revolution. Voltaire's quote appeared in *Foreign Affairs*, January-February 1995, p. 75. Churchill's quotation is from his *History of the English-Speaking Peoples*, a one-volume edition arranged by Henry Steele Commager, p. 262.

7. The letter to Parliament is included in Leopold Launitz-Schurer Jr.'s *Loyal Whigs and Revolutionaries: The Making of the Revolution in New York, 1765-1776*, pp. 23-4.

8. For the Girard-Astor purchase of 1812 war bonds, see Charles R. Geisst, *Wall Street: A History*, p. 20.

9. On Randall's home and the fire of September 1776, see *Valentine's Manual*, 1866, p. 774. For differing views about the cause of the fire see Thomas Fleming, *Liberty*, pp. 202, 205; and Edwin G. Burrows and Mike Wallace, *Gotham: A History of New York City to 1898*, pp. 241-2.

10. The Thomas Randall from Boston is identified by Philip Chadwick Foster Smith in *Empress of China*, p. 60.

11. In his article about slavery in New York in the *William and Mary Quarterly*, James G. Lydon reports on the owners and adventures of the schooner *Catherine*.

12. In *The Forgotten Trade*, Nigel Tattersfield writes about an Englishman from Weymouth named Thomas Randall who was a smuggler and a slaver early in the eighteenth century. See pp. 225 and 419.

13. Hamilton's threat appears in Thomas Fleming's *Liberty*, p. 379.

14. The letter from the president to Captain Randall, dated May 2, 1789, is in the files of The Marine Society of the City of New York. Washington had become an honorary member of the society in 1783. Volumes 2 and 3 of James Grant Wilson's *The Memorial History of the City of New York* (1893) identify Thomas Randall in a variety of pre- and post-revolutionary roles. See his index. Also see Ira K. Morris, *Morris' Memorial History of Staten Island* (1900), pp. 412-4.

15. In the sixth and final thick volume of his *Iconography of Manhattan Island, 1498-1909*, I. N. Phelps Stokes includes an encyclopedic section describing the early farmlands below Harlem as shown in original grants, deeds, and other sources. For Daniel Horsmanden's investigation of the plot to burn the city, see Stokes, 5:565-71. See also Horsmanden's own account written in 1744.

16. A 17-page report about the 11 slaves freed by the Dutch and their farms was written by Christopher Moore in 1993 for the Schomburg Center for Research in Black Culture.

17. Regarding Elliot, see L. Edward Purcell, *Who Was Who in the American Revolution*; Robert A. East and Jacob Judd, eds., *The Loyalist Americans: A Focus on Greater New York*; and Stokes's *Iconography*, vol. 4.

18. About the neighborhood and the neighbors, see *Valentine's Manual*, 1864, p. 849; Thomas A. Janvier, *In Old New York*, p. 123; *New York Herald Tribune*, "The Best Paying Farm in the United States," October 19, 1924, pp. 7-9; Charles Lockwood, *Manhattan Moves Uptown*, pp. 54-5

19. Brevoort's victory over city hall is described in the 1865 edition of *Valentine's Manual*, p. 643.

20. See appendix 1 for Robert Randall's will.

GETTING UNDER WAY

The Trustees Finally Meet

Nearly five years passed between the death of Robert Richard Randall and the first recorded meeting of the Sailors' Snug Harbor Board of Trustees on April 21, 1806, in the New York City Hall office of Mayor DeWitt Clinton. Eleven weeks earlier, the state legislature had finally approved the application of the trustees for an act of incorporation. Passage of that act on February 4, 1806, was due almost entirely to the political power and acumen of Clinton—mayor, state senator, and president of the Sailors' Snug Harbor Board of Trustees.[1]

DeWitt Clinton rescued the Randall will from a dangerous legal entanglement in Albany.

In 1798, at age 28, Clinton had been elected to the New York State Legislature and in 1801 to the U.S. Senate. Two years later, he resigned from his Senate seat when Governor George Clinton, his uncle, appointed him mayor of New York. In 1805, the citizenry sent him to the state legislature for a second time. Clinton served as both mayor and state senator because dual office was not frowned upon in those days.

An early action upon his return to Albany involved the Randall will and the legal tangle that endangered it. Most of the legislators had concluded that a man could not by his will vest his estate in a permanent official body, because such a bequest created an illegal corporation.

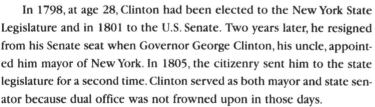

The Reverend John Rogers, "The Napoleon of New York Presbyterianism."

Had a rightful next of kin come forward to demand Randall's land and money, the will almost surely would have been declared void—but none had appeared in the years since Captain Randall's death.

Clinton took an entirely different stance and drew up a bill conferring corporate power on the offices named in the will. The bill passed, setting up the act of incorporation. If Clinton had remained in Washington, D.C., would there have been a Sailors' Snug Harbor?

According to board minutes, five of the eight trustees attended that first official meeting. Along with Clinton, who presided, were Captains James Farquhar and Thomas Farmer, president and vice president of The Marine Society, the Reverend Benjamin Moore, rector of Trinity Church, and the Reverend John Rogers, rector of the First Presbyterian Church on Wall Street. Missing were Recorder Pierre C. Van Wyck, who would be on hand for the second meeting May 28; Chancellor John Lansing Jr.; and Cornelius Ray, president of the chamber of commerce. The latter two had reasonable excuses for their absence. Because the capital of the state had been moved from New York City to Albany, Lansing was unable to be a frequent attendee. The chamber of commerce was defunct, crushed by Jefferson's Embargo Act that outlawed all foreign trade and by internal bickering stemming from the War of 1812. No chamber meetings were held between 1806 and 1817. Even so, Ray attended a number of Harbor sessions during that long hiatus.

The board of trustees was fortunate in its formative years to have members of distinction and longevity in its maritime and clerical chairs and to benefit from the civic prowess of Clinton who was mayor for 10 of 12 years, Federalist candidate in the 1812 presidential election won by James Madison, governor twice (1817-21 and 1825-28), and the visionary most responsible for building the Erie Canal.

Captain Farquhar, president of The Marine Society from 1786 to 1825, was a trustee for 19 years. His three successors in office—John Whetten, a member by marriage of the wealthy Brevoort family who became the first governor of the Harbor in 1833; Charles H. Marshall, director of the first great line of packet ships, the Black Ball Line; and John A. Ferrier—served as trustees until 1876.

Almost from the day in 1763 that the Reverend John Rogers took the pulpit of the First Presbyterian Church, he preached the Whig virtues of republicanism and independence along with theological doctrine. When Rogers and his congregation were driven from the city by the British occupation, he became a chaplain with the Continental Army. Following the evacuation of the British, the pastor returned to Wall Street to find his church, used as a stable by the Redcoats, in need of extensive repair. Trinity generously allowed its nonconformist neighbor to hold services in St. George's, the Episcopal chapel on Beekman Street. At the celebration of the two-hundredth anniversary of First Presbyterian in December 1916, John Rogers was remembered as "the Napoleon of New York Presbyterianism. It was he who marshaled its forces, led its advance, won its triumphs, and endowed it with a prestige which it has never lost." On the recommendation of Benjamin Franklin who was working in London on a trade treaty in 1784, the regents of the University of Edinburgh conferred the degree of doctor of divinity on Rogers.[2] Even more unusual than the honor itself was the fact that its bestowal was inspired by Franklin, a man not in the habit of burning incense before theologians. Rogers served as pastor and Harbor trustee until his death in 1808. His successor, the Reverend Samuel Miller, resigned to become a founding professor at the Princeton Theological Seminary. The Reverend William Wirt Phillips, who ministered to First Presbyterian and served as Harbor trustee from 1826 until 1865, led First Presbyterian in 1846 from Wall Street to lower Fifth Avenue and a Gothic Revival edifice that remains one of the glories of Greenwich Village. William Paxton Miller and Howard Duffield guided the church and the Harbor into the second decade of the twentieth century.

At Trinity, the Anglican clergy faced a dilemma because of their oath of allegiance to the British Crown.[3] The Reverend Charles Inglis, named rector in 1777, had written a point-by-point refutation of Thomas Paine's *Common Sense* in a pamphlet called *The True Interest of America Impartially Stated*. Forced to resign in 1783, Inglis—a widower—and his two young children were among 32,030 loyalists who requested evacuation from the port of New York. Like Inglis, who was to become the first Anglican bishop of a British colony, the overwhelming majority planned to start over in Nova Scotia and New Brunswick. Only 204 families returned to England.[4] Inglis was replaced at Trinity by Benjamin Moore, assistant minister and father of Clement Clarke Moore—author of *A Visit from St. Nicholas*. Moore, in turn, had to step aside in favor of the Reverend Samuel Provoorst, a patriot who had resigned from Trinity and moved upstate when the troops of Sir Henry Clinton occupied New York City in September 1776. Moore stayed on as an assistant. Provoorst, named the first Episcopal bishop of the state of New York, retired in 1800 after the death of his wife. On Provoorst's recommendation, Moore was again elected rector as well as bishop. He was also president of Columbia College from 1802 to 1811. The Reverend John Henry Hobart served Trinity Church and Harbor until 1830. A founder of General Theological Seminary, he was credited with creating a new sense of mission for a congregation that suffered from a loyalist hangover because it had sided with a king rather than independence. The Reverend William Berrian oversaw the construction in 1845 of the third Trinity Church to stand at the head of Wall Street. The Reverend Morgan Dix, son of New York Governor John A. Dix and a prolific writer, was rector and trustee for more than four decades beginning in the Civil War.

1806 seal with the motto, Portum Petimus Fesse ("Wearily, we seek a haven") and the artist's fanciful view of a Sailors' Snug Harbor still in the planning stage.

At that initial meeting on April 21, 1806, the trustees established bylaws for the new corporation, commissioned a seal for the institution, and formed committees that would prepare reports on the property belonging to the Harbor and on a monument to be erected in honor of Robert Richard Randall. John Murray, a past president of the chamber of commerce, had acted as treasurer of the estate from Randall's death until the Harbor's incorporation. In June 1806, he turned $6,208.72 over to the board. How much of this represented income from the real estate is not known, but it appears that Murray leased out a number of lots. By the third meeting on July 7, the trustees were ready to invest in bank and business stocks and to authorize land leases. One of the first of the new leases on the downtown property went to Captain Farquhar for an annual rent of $750.

The monthly meeting routine of discussing investments and leases was broken at the April 6, 1807, session when the board's attorney Jacob Radcliff reported that, because Paul Randall had become an "absent debtor" in France, his creditors had instituted a lawsuit against the trustees. The board accepted Radcliff's recommendation that the money—$1,631.81—be paid "into the Court and disposed by the Chancellor as he sees fit." A payment—no sum noted—was also authorized to the widow of George Brewerton (née Catherine Randall).

Between November 21, 1809, and February 19, 1814, the board was unable to gather a legal quorum of five members despite "repeated attempts," according to a petition from the trustees to the state legislature. The petition explained that the chancellor had refused to accept his role as a trustee "from scruples of official delicacy," that the chamber of commerce was defunct, that the senior Episcopal minister had been too ill to attend meetings, and that there were doubts about the identity of the senior Presbyterian minister since the resignation of the Reverend Samuel Miller. The trustees added that the quorum problem could be resolved by amending the law to reduce from five to three the number of trustees needed to form a legal group.

The legislature declined to reduce the size of a quorum, but it did make it a matter of law that the rector of Trinity Church (or his assistant in case of illness) and the minister of First Presbyterian Church on Wall Street were the legal trustees. This ruling, amending the original act of incorporation, also obligated the trustees to file annual reports with the legislature and the city's common council.

Two decades later when the Harbor board was still hampered by quorum troubles, it asked the legislature to authorize the addition of three "city freeholders" as coequal trustees for terms of three years. The bylaw change was approved by the legislature and signed by Governor William L. Marcy, the Tammany Tiger who originated the term "spoils system." A letter from trustee G. W. Lawrence, mayor of New York at the time, to Governor Marcy explains why the board refused to sign on to the new bylaw. "The Act," Lawrence wrote, "not only provided for the appointment of three additional Trustees . . . but also that the Legislature shall have the right, at any time, to alter, modify, or repeal the [terms of the will]. Acceptance of the Act would be an acknowledgment . . . that the Legislature would have the right to pass Laws authorizing any additional number of Trustees or otherwise to take the Trust entirely out of the hands of those designated in the will."

In January 1817, in answer to a formal demand from the common council for the annual financial statement, the trustees reported "an income for 1816 of $6,659.92 and a balance to the good in leases and securities of $56,033.53." Captain Randall's estate had more than doubled in value since 1801.

Jacob Radcliff, who had succeeded DeWitt Clinton as mayor, called a special meeting of the trustees for February 21, 1817, to consider "a subject that had been for some time deliberated"—whether to ask the legislature to modify the Randall will so that Sailors' Snug Harbor could be built in a place other than the Randall farm, whose land value had soared as the city had expanded. Broadway had already been extended to the southern boundary of the farm. Radcliff opened the meeting by reading a letter from Governor Daniel Tomkins. Having heard that some trustees had expressed a desire to erect their hospital for old seamen on Staten Island, the governor—himself a resident of Staten Island—offered "to procure for them gratuitously, a lot not less than ten acres in extent on the margin of the bay," between Fort Diamond and the quarantine ground. The trustees read and discussed a draft of an appeal to the legislature to allow the hospital to be built on Staten Island. For reasons unknown, this all-important issue was allowed to languish.

Relocation—sparked by the need to decide whether to renew the original leases now coming to term—came off the back burner early in 1823. A draft of an application seeking legislative permission to change the site of the proposed hospital noted that the ground required for buildings and yard "would materially encroach on the plot of twenty-one acres, and diminish not only the number of building lots, but depreciate their value." Continuing with a "not-in-my-backyard" theme, the application stated:

> A Seaman's Hospital in the heart of the city may be in some measure regarded as a nuisance to the immediate neighborhood. No respectable family would incline to live in the vicinity of a Lazaretto. The pensioners must be in a degree imprisoned, subject to the strictest discipline, to prevent them from wandering abroad and annoying the community. However rigid the rules such consequences will inevitably attend the natural indulgence of permitting them singly or in numbers to make excursions for air and exercise. In spite of any restriction they would become street beggars to acquire the means of intoxication.

The report was written by John Pintard, whose title of clerk cloaked his true duties as an effective executive secretary.

The board extended its land leases for two years while awaiting a decision by the legislature. Some leases were sold. Peter Cooper, who kept a grocery store on the corner of Stuyvesant Street and the Bowery, paid the Harbor $1,300 for a parcel of land on Sand Hill that included two houses with stables, a schoolhouse, and several other buildings. Cooper was on his way to his first fortune.[5]

The trustees filed a new application in Albany in January 1825. It differed in an important way from its predecessor—it sought permission to buy or exchange small parcels of land to give each lot a proper front and to make the 21 acres conform to the streets and avenues laid out in the city commissioners' grid plan of 1811. For the first time, the trustees mentioned possible hospital sites in Manhattan on or near the banks of the East or North Rivers. Before responding to the new application, the legislature sought an opinion from Attorney General Samuel Walcott about the legality of altering the terms of Randall's will. Walcott cleared the way for approval by noting that "whenever Courts of Equity have been called upon to act in the regulation or distribution of charitable donations, they have always considered that the principal design of the donor was to confer a benefit upon the objects of his beneficence; and that the advancement of the general purposes of the charity was of more importance than the particular means of administering it."

Finally, on April 8, 1828, the legislature approved the trustees' petition to change the future site of the Sailors' Snug Harbor from the Randall farm so that its 20-some acres could be subdivided into 253 leasehold lots covering most of the 10 square city blocks between Fourth and Fifth Avenues, Waverly Place, and Tenth Street.

Up to this point, and for another five years, not a single seaman had benefited from the generous bequest for the benefit of ancient, decrepit, and worn out mariners. What follows recounts the legal and family wrangling that prevented commencement of the good works.

Litigation: Collateral Heirs

The carefully crafted will of Robert Richard Randall came surprisingly close to nullification in the 1820s as it came under legal siege by contenders who claimed to have vital ties to the Randall family. On January 28, 1822, the trustees received "The memorial of Stephen R. Brown," stating that he was the legal heir to one-third of the Randall estate. Brown based his claim on the will of his grandfather, Stephen Richards of New Jersey, who died during the Revolutionary War. According to Brown, his grandfather divided his estate into three parts—one-third for his mother, Mrs. Brown; one-third to the wife of Thomas Randall, Gertrude Crooke, and her sister; and one-third to a relative in Bermuda. Captain Randall was appointed executor, Brown wrote, but failed to fulfill his duty to the heirs. Brown claimed that at Randall's death, the Captain had turned over to his son and daughter

This obelisk in the graveyard of St. Paul's honors the Irish patriot, Thomas Addis Emmet, who died while defending Randall's will against legal challenge.

the part of the grandfather's estate that belonged to the heirs of Mrs. Brown. Brown's request for a meeting with the trustees was turned over to Richard Riker, a member of the board in his role as recorder of the city of New York. Riker, reminding the trustees that young Randall had been dead for nearly 20 years and that Stephen Richards had died some 40 years ago, argued, "To authorize the allowance of a claim under these circumstances would require . . . not only the most clear and unexcep-

Daniel Webster, orator and statesman, represented the Bishop of Nova Scotia in his attempt before the U.S. Supreme Court to overthrow Randall's will.

tional proof, but the sanction of a court." He advised the trustees not to meet Brown and to inform him that they would recognize his claims only if directed to do so by a court.

Although Brown's case seemed to fade away at the time, he would return as a claimant at a later, more dangerous legal period for the Harbor. In a historical sense, the most interesting bit of information in Brown's memorial was his demand that "one white lead factory" and "one paper hanging factory" be turned over to him—evidence that the trustees had been forced to accept lease-hold tenants who would be undesirable in years to come.

In November 1826, a litigant with greater ambition and determination, and more money and eminence than Brown served the trustees with papers demanding the entire Randall estate. He was Bishop John Inglis of Nova Scotia—son of Charles Inglis, former rector of Trinity Church who, after the Revolution, settled in Nova Scotia as the first colonial bishop of the Church of England.[6] More important, his mother was the former Margaret Crooke, a cousin of Thomas Randall's wife Gertrude Crooke. Inglis argued that he and the late Randall children, Robert Richard and Catherine, shared a common ancestor in one John Crooke. Now, there being no living kin of Thomas Randall, Inglis claimed the estate on the ground that he was the only collateral heir to Robert Richard. Along with Bishop Inglis's claim for Minto, separate suits were filed against the Randall properties in lower Manhattan. These were brought in the names of John Inglis, Stephen R. Brown, and William Crooke, an Inglis cousin.

Surely, the bishop's attempt to take over the Minto estate shocked the trustees, but one would not know this from the written records. Bishop Inglis seems to have spent a good deal of time in New York during the trial periods without causing any social disquiet. He, his wife, and two daughters, dined at the home of Philip Hone, who as mayor in 1826 was chairman of the Harbor trustees. Among the other guests were the Henry Brevoorts and the John Jacob Astors. In addition, the bishop was a cordial correspondent of the Reverend John Henry Hobart—rector of Trinity Church and Harbor trustee—and of Chancellor James Kent—legal consultant to the trustees and himself a member of the board.

Inglis v. Trustees was tried in the Circuit Court of the United States for the Southern District beginning on November 2, 1826. Inglis was represented by David B.T. Ogden, T.J. Oakley, and Charles F. Grim—three preeminent members of the New York bar. The trustees countered with a remarkable lineup of legal all-stars headed by Thomas Addis Emmet, a hero of the 1798 Irish rebellion in which Catholics and Presbyterians united against the Ascendancy Anglicans in a failed bid for independence.[7] Emmet, whose younger brother Robert was hanged by the British for leading still another rebellion in 1803, won release from British prison on condition that he remain in exile forever. He returned to France, where he had attempted to interest Napoleon in an invasion of Ireland. Finding the French no longer interested in Irish freedom, Emmet moved with his family to New York City in 1804. Eloquent and erudite, with degrees from Dublin's Trinity College and Edinburgh University, Emmet developed an outstanding law practice in which he gained fame pleading for Irish causes and the liberty of escaped slaves. He served as attorney general of New York State and was a frequent advocate before the U.S. Supreme Court.

The legislature, which was interested in "the prosperity and success of so noble a charity as that of the Sailors' Snug Harbor," as well as the legal issue of loyalist rights, assigned state attorney general Samuel A. Wolcott to assist in the defense. Also serving on the defense team were Martin Van Buren, who would become the eighth president of the United States in 1837, and William Slosson, well known in local court circles for his aggressiveness. In reserve was William Wirt, attorney general of the United States from 1817 to 1829. On special retainer was Chancellor James Kent, who was generally regarded as the foremost legal mind of the day.

The trials were heard by U.S. District Judge Samuel R. Betts and Smith Thompson, Justice of the U.S. Supreme Court. (In those days, members of the U.S. Supreme Court sometimes sat as federal circuit court judges.)

Tragically, the proceedings were interrupted on November 14 when

William Wirt, Attorney General for two presidents, opposed Webster.

Chief Justice John Marshall's Court decided in favor of Wirt and the Harbor trustees.

Emmet was felled by apoplexy. He died within a few hours. Court was recessed until after his burial in the churchyard of St. Mark's in the Bowery. Five years later, friends raised a 30-foot granite obelisk to Emmet's memory in the churchyard of St. Paul's Chapel near the corner of Broadway and Fulton Street. Many New Yorkers mistake the obelisk for the burial site.

Voluminous testimony led only to deadlock when the two judges divided on how to charge the jury. There were two principal points of divergence. First, was John Inglis barred from inheriting land in New York under the State's Act of 1779 against Tory property owners even though he was only four or five years of age when he fled his native land with his loyalist father on Evacuation Day? Second, was the will of Catherine (Randall) Brewerton sufficient to dispose of any collateral claim by Bishop Inglis or others? Similarly, could collateral claims be made through the estate of Paul Randall?

The second point had been inserted into the trial by the defense to break Inglis's claim of legal descent should the court pronounce him an American citizen. This point was of particular interest to the trustees, who wanted a decision that would stop forever suits by self-professed collateral heirs.

In March 1829, the appeal for guidance on these questions came before the six-member U.S. Supreme Court, presided over by Chief Justice John Marshall. The trustees were represented by Wirt and Wolcott, and Daniel Webster had joined David B. Ogden as counsel for Inglis. No one was a more formidable litigator before the Court than the great Webster.[8] Not only had he appeared before the tribunal more frequently than any other member of the bar, but he was on the friendliest of terms with most of the justices, including John Marshall, with whom he had shared a boarding-house breakfast table early in his career.

In a different way, Wirt was an unusual figure in the annals of American jurisprudence.[9] He was the author of one of the nation's first best-sellers, *The Letters of the British Spy*, witty observations on the manners and customs of the genteel South. In addition, he had been prosecutor in the treason trial of Aaron Burr. Serving under Presidents James Monroe and John Quincy Adams, Wirt was the first U.S. attorney general to make a systematic practice of preserving his official opinions so that they might serve as precedents for his successors. As was the custom while holding office, he maintained a highly successful private practice in the state courts of Maryland and Virginia.

The 54 pages of written text about the issues included a lengthy debate among the justices over the validity of the will. One question, for example, explored what the ramifications would be, had Randall named the members of the trust in their personal rather than official capacities. All this legal scrutiny resulted in a decision on January 2, 1830, favoring Sailors' Snug Harbor. On a three-to-two vote, the justices decided that the bishop was an alien who could not inherit real estate under New York State law. The minority view held that because Inglis had been born between July 4 and September 15, 1776—the period when New York City was controlled by the Continental Congress—he was an American and entitled to inherit. In the opinion of Marshall and Justices Smith Thompson and Gabriel Duval, Inglis was an Englishman; before he could inherit property in New York State he would have had to declare himself an American, which he never did. What slight validity the Inglis claim may have had was overridden, the Court ruled, by the Forfeiture Acts of the state legislature directed against Tory property owners. On the matter of collateral claims, the vote was four-to-one for the trustees.

The sixth, Bushrod Washington, nephew of George Washington, died before the votes were cast. Justice Washington's death led Webster and Ogden to seek to open the case for reargument with a double-edged claim. First, the hearing had been conducted by six justices but voted upon by only five. "Of these three were against the demandant . . . a minority of the whole court." The second claim came as a surprise—"a femme coverte," as the sister of Bishop Inglis was described in an affidavit. However, there was nothing mysterious about her as the identifying legal term may have implied to nonmembers of the bar. Simply put, she was a married woman whose husband controlled her properties. The affidavit added: "She is not subject to the disability of alienism and may therefore maintain a suit to recover the property in dispute." Wirt's rejoinder warned that allowing reargument would set a precedent "which would render every decision of the court uncertain." Marshall agreed and rejected the appeal.

Webster was upset. At the end of the trial, he wrote to his son Ezekiel that he had "made a greater exertion" in this case than any since his first appearance before the U.S. Supreme Court 10 years earlier. And, he added, it was unlikely that he would ever make such an effort again.

Meanwhile, the Harbor trustees had won all the cases involving the lower-Manhattan properties in the state supreme court and circuit court. The trustees were free at last to seek a site for the Sailors' Snug Harbor and to get on with the business of becoming a principal landlord to New Yorkers.

Notes

1. As Dorothie Bobbe shows in the 1962 edition of *DeWitt Clinton*, there might not have been a Sailors' Snug Harbor without Clinton. In the introduction to that edition, Henry Steele Commanger says Clinton gave New York "the best administration it was to enjoy until the advent of Fiorello La Guardia." The 1933 edition of Bobbe's book is much briefer and contains no mention of Randall's will.

2. A succinct account of the congregation's role in what Horace Walpole called the "Presbyterian rebellion" can be found in a six-page pamphlet available at the rear of the church. A report about the two hundredth anniversary celebration that includes Benjamin Franklin's recommendation is in the church's archives.

3. See Clifford P. Morehouse, *Trinity: Mother of Churches*.

4. See Philip Ranlet, *The New York Loyalists*, p. 173.

5. See Edward Mack, *Peter Cooper: Citizen of New York*, pp. 58, 100.

6. The Fort Schuyler archives carry full accounts of the litigation.

7. For Thomas Addis Emmet, see Morgan Dix, ed., *A History of the Parish of Trinity Church in the City of New York*, 4:68; R. F. Foster, Modern Ireland: 1600–1972, p. 265.

8. For Daniel Webster, see Claude Moore Fuess, *Daniel Webster*, 2:226, 2:234, 2:257, and letter to Ezekiel, 2:299.

9. For William Wirt, see *Dictionary of American Biography*; and Fuess, *Daniel Webster*, 2:226.

RANDALL'S PLAN FULFILLED: STATEN ISLAND

By the winter of 1830, almost three decades after Captain Randall wrote has will, the trustees of Sailors' Snug Harbor were finally free to turn his vision into reality. Captains John Whetten and William Whitlock, trustees from The Marine Society, had been assigned to find a site for the Harbor that would allow the old seamen "to daily witness ships passing in and out of the port, a situation which would gladden, if not prolong, the remnant of their day." Although Governor Daniel Tomkins's offer of 10 free acres of Staten Island shoreline as a site for the hospital had lapsed with his death in 1825, the island's rural seascape remained a choice location. In 1833, young Cornelius Vanderbilt introduced regular ferry service between Staten Island and Manhattan. Soon Staten Island was to become a summer retreat for wealthy families from New York and the South. A mixed population of year-round residents, including a colony of free blacks who harvested oysters from the rich offshore waters, lived on small farms and in pleasing villages such as New Brighton, which would become the well-to-do neighbor of Sailors' Snug Harbor. Not only would the locality and the view be congenial, but it served the requirements of a prevailing medical theory that recommended situating health-care facilities away from the stresses of urban life.[1]

In May 1831, the trustees purchased the 130-acre Staten Island farm of Isaac Houseman for $10,000. The farm's 1,600 feet of north

Flags and bunting drape Main Hall on its 75th anniversary in 1908 during the Harbor's Golden Age. Captain Robert Richard Randall is buried beneath the granite obelisk.

shore footage overlooked the Upper Bay and the tranquil Kill Van Kull with views of a distant Manhattan and a bucolic Bayonne, New Jersey. Subsequently the trustees purchased an additional 21 acres, which included a bountiful spring, for $6,000. They leased another 36 acres of excellent woodland.

Greek Revival Comes to Staten Island

Newspaper advertisements in the spring of 1831 invited proposals for a brick or stone building that would accommodate 200 seaman along with "the necessary offices, kitchen, bakery, storerooms, etc." A $50 premium was offered for the best plan. According to trustee minutes and the treasurer's accounts, the winning design was submitted by Minard Lafever, an ambitious 33-year-old upstate carpenter who had recently moved to New York City, where he would become a noted architect. Over the next two decades, following his initial architectural venture at Sailors' Snug Harbor, Lafever designed many churches and private residences marked by dignity and restraint. Among works attributed to him are two lower-Manhattan landmarks, the Old Merchant's House off the Bowery (1832) and the Church of St. James near Chatham

Neptune Ceiling, part of the building's unusual maritime ornamentation.

The main hall of the original dormitory soars to a spectacular circular skylight.

Square (1835-37), in what is now Chinatown. Many of his finest buildings still stand in Brooklyn Heights and nearby Cobble Hill, including Holy Trinity Church and Packer Collegiate Institute.

Lafever's great influence as a working architect was matched by his skill as the author of a series of remarkable pattern books for carpenter-builders that described sound construction methods and illustrated the newly fashionable ornamental detail of the Greek Revival style. The fronts and interiors of many a Greek Revival row house in Greenwich Village and Brooklyn were surely inspired by what entrepreneurial carpenters discovered in *The Modern Builder's Guide* and *The Beauties of Modern Architecture*. Lafever's guides helped shape the Greek Revival movement throughout the country. Perhaps not by coincidence, the popular books came along at the very time that Americans were becoming Grecophiles, identifying with the democracy of ancient Greece and the modern Greeks' fight for independence from Turkey during the 1820s.

However, Lafever was unknown when the trustees chose him to build their home for old seamen. Tradition, in fact, gave credit for Snug Harbor's early Greek Revival buildings to Martin E. Thompson, an established architect who had already designed two highly regarded Wall Street structures, the Branch Bank of the United States and the Merchants' Exchange.

Proper attribution was finally established in 1976 by Barnett Shepherd, an architectural historian then writing *Sailors' Snug Harbor 1801-1976*. His 16-page article in the *Journal of the Society of Architectural Historians* reviewed the work of Lafever and Thompson and the Harbor's records. Shepherd concluded, "The Martin Thompson attribution is without basis, and the authorship of the buildings can be ascribed to Minard Lafever. . . . The design of the buildings, together with the evidence of documents bearing Lafever's name, makes the attribution beyond reasonable question."

According to Shepherd, the attribution of the Snug Harbor buildings to Thompson in Talbot Hamlin's *Greek Revival Architecture in America* (1944) was based on misinformation provided by Thompson's descendants. Shepherd also suggested that the confusion may have been due to the fact that another builder with a similar name, Samuel Thomson, had been associated with the work from the very start. Lafever worked on his original building through the first year of construction, providing detailed drawings and ordering building supplies.

There is no explanation of why he left the project a year before it was completed in August 1833. Whatever the reason, Samuel Thomson & Son, who had repaired properties on Broadway and Eighth Street in 1831 for the Harbor trustees, was engaged to finish the work. In 1840 and 1842, the Thomsons constructed the west and east wings of Lafever's Greek Revival row.

Among the supplies ordered by Lafever was marble that had been quarried, cut, shaped, and numbered by Sing Sing prisoners, then shipped down the Hudson on barges to the newly constructed wharf at Sailors' Snug Harbor. Use of convict-quarried stone was a popular cost-saving maneuver that was soon to lead to major problems with organized labor. The target of the Stone Cutters' Guild was the newly opened University of the City of New York—or New York University (NYU) as it is known today—that was to be the Harbor's neighbor on Washington Square. Convict-quarried stone, used to construct NYU's University Building, set off a riot and four days of confrontation between workers and the National Guard.[2] The NYU building would be the last building in New York to be built with marble quarried by prison labor.

On Staten Island, the cornerstone of what was to be the central building in a complex of five Greek temples was laid on October, 21 1831, by Chancellor of the State of New York Reuben Walworth.[3] The full board and, according to board minutes, "a number of the most respectable citizens of New York and vicinity" attended the ceremonies. Remarks and prayers "appropriate to the occasion" were made by Mayor Walter Brown and the Reverends William Berrigan and William W. Phillips.

Nearly 22 months passed before the first building of the temple row opened on August 1, 1833. Lafever's inspiration for the buildings had been found in illustrations of the Temple of Illysus in the *Antiquities of Athens* (1762) by the English authors James Stuart and Nicholas Revett and in James Elmes's rendering of the London Orphan Asylum in *Metropolitan Improvements* (1827).

The main façade of the two-story brick building, with high basement and attic, is sheathed in marble. Its portico of eight monumental Ionic columns carries a full entablature and a shallow pediment. The entrance is approached by a flight of stone steps extending the width of the temple front. Inside were 34 living and working spaces. The

central hall and gallery, running the length of the building and soaring to a delicate dome with circular skylight, is distinguished to this day by unusual nautical ornament. A balustrade encircles it on the second floor. The north rooms on the right of the central hall were offices for the governor and clerk; rooms on the left of the hall served as reception rooms and library.

The Randall Memorial Church and its neighbor, the Music Hall, were both completed in 1893.

A few weeks before the building's opening, the following notice was sent to newspapers and waterfront church groups: "Sailors' Snug Harbor will be in readiness to receive aged seamen on the first day of August next. Applications will be received on and after the 4th of July."

Old Seamen in Their Final Harbor

Thirty-seven retired seamen neatly dressed in blue jackets and white trousers attended the opening ceremonies as the first resident-beneficiaries of Captain Randall's will. About one-third were described as crippled, mostly by rheumatism or rupture; six were listed as decrepit; four had lost a leg; and two were blind. The average age was 58, ranging from 23 to 75. Of the men, 18 were American; 9 were English; and the others were Irish, Scots, Dutch, Prussian, and French.

*Aerial view of Sailors'
Snug Harbor, 1936.
Randall Memorial
Church and the music
hall are set back to the
far left of the Greek
Revival dormitories.
Immediately behind
the front-five buildings
are two additional
dormitories and the
dining hall. The hospital
complex is in the far
rear. Behind it is the
enormous sanitarium.
Far to the right, in
line with the front
buildings, is the gover-
nor's mansion.*

No one was shut out of the institution because of race, creed, or color, although habitual alcoholics and those with contagious disease or immoral character were banned. The all-important requirements were 10 years or more in the crews of ocean-going vessels, including 5 years under the flag of the United States, or incapacitation incurred while serving at sea. Captains and mates, as well as ordinary seamen, were welcome if they were aged, decrepit, or worn out.

The annual cost to feed, clothe, and care for each resident was estimated to be $88.50, not counting the overall price of fuel, which was approximately $900. Costs included monthly wages for a steward ($15), matron ($10), cook ($10), and three nurses ($7 each).

In the summer of 1834, a granite obelisk honoring Robert Richard Randall was placed in front of the new home for old sailors. The captain's remains were conveyed from a crypt at St. Mark's in the Bowery and buried under the monument. Originally, Randall had been buried on his farm, but the casket had been moved in 1825 to make way for the construction of Eighth Street. An intriguing, but unanswered, aspect of Captain Randall's burial is found in the correspondence of the Reverend Morgan Dix, rector of Trinity Church and a Harbor Trustee for 46 years. In reply to an 1877 letter inquiring if Robert Richard was buried in the family's Trinity churchyard vault, Dix noted: "I have recently heard a statement that Captain Randall, by his own orders, was buried on his farm in an erect position with his back towards the East. Do you know whether the tradition is a current one?"

The Harbor Expands

By the end of 1834, 83 seamen had been admitted to the Harbor. Two had died and 20 had gone off for various reasons, but it was clear to the trustees that the population of Building C, as it was called in the construction plan, would soon reach its limit of 200. Identical buildings, D and E, were built almost simultaneously between 1840 and 1842 as dormitories. Equal in size to the main building, each showed three-bay facades with simple stoops leading to the first floor's central bay entrance. Small Ionic porches were added in 1880 during construction of Buildings A and E, the final dormitories in this Greek Revival row. These are fronted by six-column porticos with full-width flights of stone steps. The five buildings are connected by one-story brick and windowed passageways that Lafever called hyphens.

By midcentury, two shorefront mansions for the governor and the physician, a chapel, a hospital, and a large dining hall had been erected. The hospital would expand a number of times including an 1898 addition of a huge x-shaped sanitarium. Randall Memorial Church, said to be a one-sixth-scale replica of St. Paul's Cathedral in London, and a music hall that would have been at home on Broadway opened in the 1890s. A handsome recreation hall and library erected in 1918 completed the construction phase of the Sailors' Snug Harbor facility on Staten Island.

In all, 55 buildings, including two more dormitories, cottages for staff members, a powerhouse, and a morgue, had been built on the former Houseman farm. Along with the structures of marble, mortar, and brick, were an imposing pedestal and bronze statue of Robert Richard Randall by Augustus Saint Gaudens; a Neptune fountain; a Victorian gazebo; and an impressive iron fence that surrounds most of the property and its acres of flower gardens, great lawns, shrubs, and bushes; stands of pine and elm; plus the farmland that fed nearly 1,000 "snugs" at the turn of the twentieth century. Six acres had been given over to a graveyard, where the remains of some 8,000 mariners rest.

The patrimony that underwrote this unmatched example of private philanthropic enterprise came, of course, from what had been Randall's farm in Manhattan.

Notes

1. Carol von Pressentin Wright's *Blue Guide: New York* describes Staten Island in the early nineteenth century as does Henry G. Steinmeyer's *Staten Island: 1524-1898.*

2. On the stonecutter's riot, see Rick Beard and Leslie Cohen Berlowitz, eds., *Greenwich Village: Culture and Counterculture*, pp. 200-3.

3. For the Greek Revival Row, see Harmon H. Goldstone and Martha Dalrymple, *History Preserved: A Guide to New York City Landmarks and Historic Districts*; Barbarlee Diamonstein, *Landmarks of New York*; and Barnett Shepherd's article in *The Journal of the Society of Architectural Historians.*

Manhattan: Moving Uptown

Renewed Prosperity

Whenen New York's elegant city hall opened for business and politics in 1811 in what had been "The Fields," its southern and side walls were sheathed in white marble; its northern rear was constructed of cheaper brownstone because its builders believed it was unlikely that Manhattan would grow beyond this uptown point for many years to come.[1] Presumably, the city fathers who made the brownstone decision were unfamiliar with the 1811 street plan developed by a three-member commission that had been appointed by the state legislature in 1807 and their surveyor John Randel Jr. (no relation to the Randalls). The plan's grid pattern of streets and avenues stretched all the way from Houston Street to 155th Street.[2] The commissioners might well have been visionaries, because commerce in New York had not yet recovered from President Thomas Jefferson's ill-considered embargo of 1807 to 1809 against Britain and France and from the War of 1812. By the time news of a treaty ending the second war with England arrived in New York on February 11, 1815, the blockaded city was in severe depression. Holding long pent-up ambitions, city merchants and mariners responded at once to the opportunities that accompanied peace. Good fortune played a role, too, in the rise of New York as the New World emporium for trade and finance.

In the 1820s, the 21-acre Randall farm, squarely in the path of a fast-expanding city, was divided into 253 income-producing building lots that became Manhattan's most elegant neighborhood. Lease rents from row upon row of townhouses underwrote the purchase of 130 acres on Staten Island, site of Sailors' Snug Harbor—America's first and grandest home for aging seamen. (Numbers within the building lots are street addresses.)

The Black Ball Line's James Monroe *making the first regularly scheduled merchant sailing trips in the history of the sea.*

Britain, unable to sell to its usual customers because of war with Napoleon as well as the United States, had accumulated a huge inventory of woolen and cotton goods and manufactures of all kinds. The blockade, tighter against New York than other ports, had left the city's shelves bare. This double problem had an obvious answer—the British "dumped" their products in New York. For weeks, ships by the dozen sailed from British ports to unload at South Street docks.[3] Normally, even the emptiest market would soon be glutted, sending the merchant ships on to other ports. However, a cagey maneuver by the city's auction houses, who profited even with below-value prices, kept merchandise and customers flowing into New York. They had sponsored special legislation requiring that all items put up for auction must be sold, a move that guaranteed continuous bargains.[4] This heavy increase in business volume also transformed city merchants from jacks-of-all trades to specialists in a new kind of marketplace.

January 5, 1818, a crucial day in the history of New York trade, saw the launching of the Black Ball Line.[5] Its four fast and commodious square-rigged packet ships were to make the first regularly scheduled sailings in the history of the sea. The ships, carrying passengers and "fine freight," sailed between Liverpool and New York on a specified day each month whether "full or unfull." At precisely 10 A.M., the advertised hour, Captain James Watkinson gave the order for the *James Monroe* to cast off from the East River's Pier 23. During the 28-day voyage to England, the *James Monroe* passed another Black Baller, the *Courier*, on its way from Liverpool to Pier 23.

A dozen years earlier, Robert Fulton's North River steamboat, known to history as the *Clermont*, had introduced the world's first successful steamboat service on the Hudson River and Long Island Sound. In 1825, the Erie Canal opened the western hinterland to direct trade with New York. And because of its role as banker, broker, and shopkeeper for the antebellum South, New York had become the principal shipper of cotton to Europe. All this was making many New Yorkers very rich and the tip of Manhattan very noisy and congested.

The City Moves Uptown

In the 1820s, wealthy businessmen and their families began moving uptown, their once splendid homes on Wall Street, the Battery, and Broadway demolished or transformed by commerce. No one has described this exodus of the rich better than Philip Hone, who served as Harbor trustee while mayor in 1826. His *Diary* is a perceptive and opinionated report about the social and political life of New York during the second quarter of the nineteenth century. As a partner in his brother's auction house, he had become wealthy enough to retire in 1821, at age 41, and to move his family to a $25,000 mansion overlooking City Hall Park. By 1836, the advance of shops, hotels, and crowds, plus a price he could not turn down, impelled Hone to move to Great Jones Street, just above Bond and Bleecker Streets, in what was becoming the city's most fashionable neighborhood. According to Hone: "Almost everybody downtown is in the same predicament for all the dwelling houses are to be converted to stores. We are tempted with prices so exorbitantly high that none can resist. . . . I have turned myself out of doors, but $60,000 is a great deal of money."[6]

Philip Hone, mayor and trustee and, above all, perceptive diarist.

Noting that real estate speculation was rampant, Hone wrote: "Men in moderate circumstances have become immensely rich merely by the good fortune of owning farms of a few acres in this chosen land." Men with more than a few acres to sell, such as John Jacob Astor and Henry

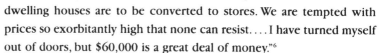

Brevoort, neighbors of Sailors' Snug Harbor, were worth millions. With the rapid approach of the city to the Randall farm, the Harbor trustees petitioned the state legislature for permission to find a new location for the sailors' home and to divide the Manhattan land into income-producing building lots. Even before the trustees received legislative approval, hills on the farm were leveled and streets laid out in conformance with the 1811 commissioners' plan. Minto, the mansion known as Sailors' Snug Harbor after the death of Randall, was torn down. Harbor trustees granted the city permission to extend Broadway, whose uptown march had been stalled since 1809 at a white fence marking the southern boundary of the Randall farm. To square a number of irregular lots along Eighth and Tenth Streets and University and Astor Places, trustees paid a total of $85,000 to the city and to neighbors Henry Brevoort and Dudley Selden. Adjacent parcels at the foot of Fifth Avenue were swapped with George P. Rogers who was developing property west of the avenue. The avenue itself had been opened by the city for development as far as Thirteenth Street in 1824. But the first of the Fifth Avenue mansions did not appear until 1834, when Henry Brevoort Jr. built his stately Georgian home on the northwest corner of Ninth Street. It was to become the center of New York's high society. With Hone as the reporter once again, some 500 ladies and gentlemen attended a masquerade ball at Brevoort's mansion in the winter of 1840. Hone, who attended as Cardinal Wolseley, judged the mansion "better calculated for such a display than any other in the city."

On February 1, 1827, Harbor leases for lots fronting on Broadway and the Bowery, each 25 feet wide and 100 feet deep, were auctioned at the Tontine Coffee House. Annual rents ranged from $130 to $150 for leases of 21 years. Seventy additional lots on Greene, Mercer, Eighth, Ninth, and Tenth Streets were ready for builders—but no construction was started because of the legal challenges of Bishop Inglis.

As the trustees complained in their annual report to the legislature in January 1829, "The law suits . . . present insurmountable obstacles to the present improvement of the properties. The parties who purchased the leases in February 1827 have refused to take them, under an impression of loss should they improve the property, and a decision be against the Trustees."

Once the U.S. Supreme Court cleared the way in 1830 for the trustees to implement the Randall will, they moved with alacrity and vision.

Washington Square
facing the Gothic towers
of the University Building
and the South Dutch
Reformed Church in
the 1860s.

Washington Square

When the Randall farm was being divided into building lots, the most valuable properties were thought to be those bordering on Broadway—the widest, handsomest thoroughfare in the city. Neither the trustees nor the Randalls before them could have foreseen that what was a marshland teeming with wildlife immediately to the south of the farm would be transformed into a parade ground and public park known as Washington Square.

One year before the Randalls bought the farm in 1790, the city had purchased seven acres of that neighboring property from the Herring family for a potter's field and an execution ground. In 1797, the city acquired approximately four additional acres from Colonel William S. Smith. The square's final acreage was purchased from Alfred Pell and the Warren estate.

Potter's Field was a busy place where wooden coffins were piled three and four deep in trenches. Before it was drained and leveled in 1826 and turned into a military parade ground, somewhere between 10,000 and 20,000 bodies had been interred. A large number were victims of yellow fever and cholera. The last of many hangings on the grounds took place in 1819. On July 8, the *Evening Post* reported that

"Rose, a black girl who had been sentenced for setting fire to a dwelling ... was executed yesterday at 2 o'clock near Potter's Field."[7] Legend has it that the 110-foot elm, still standing at the northwest entrance to the park, was a hanging tree. The story is probably untrue. Not only did the tree stand on private land until the strip of Warren property was purchased but, since the days of the Dutch, executions had been carried out on gallows.[8]

Property owners, including the trustees of Sailors' Snug Harbor, undoubtedly had a good deal to do with turning this grisly acreage into a public greensward that would be attractive for residential development. A splendid example of what a few acres of park space could mean to a neighborhood had recently been demonstrated by Trinity Church, beneficiary of a royal grant in 1705 that gave it title to 215 acres of undeveloped land that would eventually become the west side of downtown Manhattan.[9] In the early 1800s, the church drained some swampy land—near what is today the entrance to the Holland Tunnel—built a lovely chapel called St. John's at one corner of the new park, and offered 64 surrounding lots for sale. By the mid 1820s, St. John's Park was "the fairest interior portion of this city" and "the most desirable residence."

In his history of Washington Square, Luther Harris explains how in 1826 Philip Hone—mayor, president of the board of trustees of Sailors' Snug Harbor, and member of the Trinity Church vestry—earned the accolade "Father of Washington Square."[10] It was Hone who suggested enlarging and upgrading the recently vacated Potter's Field into a military parade ground named after George Washington. That suggestion, approved by the common council, saved what would eventually be a well-groomed, 13-acre open plot of land from division into building lots. Sailors' Snug Harbor paid $4,775.50 as its share of improvement expenses in the parade ground.

Hone's next contribution to the welfare of the Harbor and the city itself was to dedicate the Washington Military Parade Ground on July 4, 1826, while celebrating the nation's fiftieth birthday. Two roasted oxen, 200 hams, and garnishments moistened by "a quarter-mile of barreled beer" plus parades and fireworks attracted some 10,000 of the citizenry despite rain. Many of the revelers, if well heeled, would build or buy houses near the parade ground in coming years.

Within 12 months of the grand dedication of the parade ground, a row of eight Federal-style, double-dormer houses was being built on what would become Washington Square South. The very first house on the north side of the parade ground was a mansion west of Fifth Avenue at what is now Number 20. Built in 1828–29 as the country home of George P. Rogers, it was among the last of the elegantly simple Federal-style houses that were giving way to the sophistication of Greek Revival architecture.[11]

The next houses on Washington Square North, Greek Revival mansions numbered 1 through 13, were built in 1832–33 on land leased from Sailors' Snug Harbor between Fifth Avenue and University Place. Known as "The Row" and judged by the Landmarks Preservation Commission to be "the most important and imposing block front of early Nineteenth Century town houses in the City," they were planned as a unified group with two slightly different personalities. The fluted marble columns of numbers 1 through 6 are simple Doric, and their window lintels are peaked. The columns of numbers 7 through 13 are crowned with Ionic scrolls, and the lintels are rectangular with small cornices. The three-story, high-basement houses were unified by a continuous, red-brick facade; an unbroken roofline pierced with little attic windows; grand marble porticos; 12-foot-deep front yards; and a block-long iron fence featuring Greek anthemions and frets plus intervals of lyres and obelisks.

The roofline was broken in 1884, when number 3 was enlarged into a studio building and remodeled in the fashionable Queen Anne style. In 1939, the roofline of numbers 7 through 13 was raised several feet, when the buildings were gutted and converted into a modern apartment house that occupied most of the spacious rear gardens. The Greek Revival front facade with its row of handsome doorways was saved by a public outcry against "architectural vandalism." Present-day entrance to numbers 7 through 13 is through a pergola corridor facing Fifth Avenue. The remodeling produced 70 apartments including six duplex units. In his *New York 1900*, architect Robert A. M. Stern found it "shocking" that the interiors were gutted to create conventional apartments with smallish rooms that made the original high ceilings look ridiculously tall.[12] Mantels from the destroyed interiors were given to museums, and measured drawings were made of some of the woodwork and ornamental detail. Photographs of the drawing rooms, dining rooms, and bedrooms were used by Paramount Studios in the 1949 film *The Heiress*, based on Henry James's novel *Washington Square*.

This prestigious row of houses was developed by three socially prominent businessmen, James Boorman, John Johnston, and John

"The Row," numbers 1-13 Washington Square North.

Morrison, who leased the land from Sailors' Snug Harbor. Long before zoning regulations, the Harbor and its lessees agreed upon a set of restrictions designed to attract wealthy residents and to protect against nuisances. The houses were to be "good and substantial, three or more stories . . . of brick or stone." A household stable would be allowed in the rear, but there was to be no "trade or business which may be noxious or offensive to the neighbors" such as slaughterhouses; breweries; bakeries; or factories for making glass, glue, turpentine, or ink.

Rear gardens were unusually large, stretching back to what is now the north side of Washington Mews, a private street designed to provide access to service quarters and stables. Interiors were spacious with high ceilings. Curving staircases, brightened by skylights, graced the center of each house. The usual layout showed kitchen, dining room, and storage space on the ground floor; front and rear parlors on the first floor; and bedrooms, servants' quarters, and utility space on the upper floors. For all their elegance, these houses would have neither indoor plumbing nor gaslight for at least another decade. On the other hand, each house had five to seven servants, most of them Irish-born.

Snug Harbor records do not name an architect-builder for The Row, but Samuel Thomson is cited as a likely candidate by Sarah Bradford

Landau, a professor of fine arts at New York University (NYU). Thomson was the speculator-builder of number 4 in The Row, he had worked in Manhattan for Snug Harbor in 1831, and in 1832 he superintended construction of Minard Lafever's Greek Revival buildings on Staten Island. In addition, NYU bought its land on the east side of the square from Thomson along with a brick pile that he had stored on the property. Landau asks, "Was this brick left over from the construction of his own and other houses on The Row?"[13]

Many of these wealthy residents of Washington Square North were related by blood, marriage, or business. Samuel Howland, his brother G. G. Howland, and their families lived at number 12. Samuel's daughter and her husband, famed architect Richard Morris Hunt, moved into number 2 in the 1880s. A nephew and partner in their worldwide trading firm, William Aspinwall, lived around the corner on University Place.

George Griswold, partner with his brother in the China-trade firm of N. L. &. G. Griswold—known on Wall Street as "No Loss & Great Gain"—lived at number 9. His daughter Sarah and her husband John C. Green, another China trader, bought number 10 in 1844. Pierre Lorillard, nephew of George Griswold, was a yachtsman, breeder of thoroughbreds, and the man responsible for teaching Americans to smoke Old Golds, one of the "big four" cigarette brands in its day. He and his family moved into number 8 in 1894.

Descendants of John Johnston, who built number 7 in 1832, still lived in The Row in the late 1930s. His son, John Taylor Johnston, started married life at number 7, but soon built a white marble mansion on the southwest corner of Fifth Avenue and Eighth Street. John Taylor Johnston's daughter Emily, and her husband, Robert W. DeForest, lived at number 7. Her sister Eva Johnston Coe lived at 5 East Tenth Street, next door to Lockwood DeForest, younger brother of Robert, and across the street from another of the Howlands, Benjamin J. In 1938, when they were well into their 80s, Emily and Eva attended an "evening of reminiscences" given by the Washington Square Association at the Hotel Brevoort.[14] As reported in the next day's *New York Times*, Emily recalled: "The social entertainments of long ago seem silly nowadays. Tea and coffee drinking was the custom and the couples would march around the parlors, and someone would sing 'When the Swallows Homeward Fly.'" One of Emily's teachers at Miss Green's school for girls at 2 East Eighth Street was Theodore Roosevelt's future secretary of state, Elihu Root, then working his way through law school at NYU. "He

*Skylights graced
the central staircases
in each house on
"The Row."*

never meets me now," said Emily, "but that he addresses me as 'young lady.'" Another of Miss Green's pupils was Jenny Jerome, who would become Lady Randolph Churchill and mother of Winston Churchill. Eva, reading from her grandmother's party book, reported that at one dinner alone 300 oysters were served along with chicken, duck, quail, and partridge.

The Row was home to six of the founders of NYU, whose grand Gothic Revival building would open on the east side of the square in 1835. James Talmadge, president of the university council from 1834 to

1846 and former congressman, lived at number 5. Number 2 was the address of Shepherd Knapp, an important banker. Thomas Suffern was an importer of Irish linen and a cousin of Andrew Jackson, to whom he played host at number 11. Other university council members on the block were John Johnston, John C. Green, and Samuel Howland. (Albert Gallatin—statesman, scholar, and the best known of the university's founding fathers—lived nearby on Eleventh Street.) Heads of other households on the block included Stephen Allen (number 1), commissioner of the Croton Water Works and former mayor; Thomas J. Oakley (number 4), a superior court judge for 30 years; Harry Rankin (number 3), president of Globe Insurance; Saul Alley (number 6) and John McGregor Jr. (number 8), eminent merchants; and James Boorman (number 13), one of the developers of The Row. After Boorman's death, his house was sold to William Butler Duncan who, in 1872, combined it with number 12 to form a double mansion that became known in the 1920s as Wanamaker House after its purchase by Rodman Wanamaker, son of the department store magnate.

The Row's neighbor on the east side of the park, NYU's white marble University Building, was the first example of English collegiate Gothic in the United States and an inspiration, with its towers and crenellated roofline, for many American college buildings yet to be built. In 1840, the South Dutch Reformed Church opened east of the parade ground immediately below NYU. Designed in the Gothic Revival style by Minard Lafever, its twin towers complemented those of its neighbor and gave the east side of the square a romantic, picturesque skyline. Long rows of brick residences, handsome but more modest than their northerly neighbors, lined the south and west sides.

Two years after its opening, the university was hit hard by the Panic of 1837, possibly the most severe of the many nineteenth-century recessions. Professors' salaries were reduced, and rooms were rented to professional groups and artists. The three-story interior chapel, "probably the most beautiful room of its kind in America," was taken over by the congregation of the South Dutch Reformed Church for several years while its new building was being constructed one block to the south.

Unlike Sailors' Snug Harbor, which had received its land as a gift, the university spent practically its entire bank account ($40,000) for its building site, and then went heavily into debt during construction. Harbor minutes make but a single reference to the panic. Suspension by banks of specie payments had tied up $2,000 in expected dividends.

Beyond the Square

Because the row of houses facing Washington Square still stand there to be admired, they are the best known of the 250 or so residences built on land leased from Sailors' Snug Harbor in the 1830s and 1840s "upon the terms and conditions of the leases now granted by the vestry of Trinity Church." Broadway from Astor Place to Tenth Street was lined with large, elegant homes. Blocks of attached Federal and Greek Revival houses, some faced in the newly fashionable brownstone, filled Randall's old farmland. The families of merchants, brokers, lawyers, publishers, physicians, and seven ministers (including the Reverend Jacob Abbott) made these blocks an integral part of an emerging upper-class neighborhood. The Reverend Abbott's leasehold at 262 Greene Street became a private school and, at a later date, the site of the administrative offices of Sailors' Snug Harbor. Many, if not most of these houses, were built on speculation by entrepreneurial artisans who followed designs carefully illustrated in architectural pattern books such as Minard Lafever's *The Young Builder's Guide* (1829) and *The Modern Builder's Guide* (1833).

All that remain of these buildings on Harbor land, in addition to the former Greene Street offices, The Row, and its Mews, are the buildings

Calendar art showing a peaceable harbor in 1837, the year New York was shaken by financial panic.

57

numbered 4 to 26 on the south side of Eighth Street between Fifth Avenue and University Place. Although these buildings do not look as they did when new, they are worth a visit because renovation was carried out with good taste and imagination when the trustees had them converted into apartments in 1916. These mostly five-story buildings were given smooth-stuccoed facades with decorative tile plaques, and a variety of ground-floor entrances, windows, arches, iron-rail balconies, and rooflines that give this bit of Manhattan a Mediterranean flavor.

A truer resemblance to Harbor properties, circa 1835, is found west of Sixth Avenue on Charlton Street, which has the longest unbroken row of Federal houses in the city, and next door on King and Vandam Streets.

A. T. Stewart and Ladies Mile

By the time the Harbor's 21-year leases began to come up for renewal in the 1850s, retail and revel were replacing residences on Broadway above Houston. Just south of Harbor property were newly opened hotels and halls including the fashionable New York Hotel, favorite haunt of gentry from the South; Triflers, a huge music hall; plus numerous shops and restaurants. Overshadowing all of this was the agreement by the trustees on November 21, 1855, to lease the 29 lots bounded by Broadway, Fourth Avenue, Ninth Street, and Tenth Street to Alexander Turney Stewart.

Stewart, an Irish-born Scot, opened the first of the city's great commercial palaces in 1846 at Broadway and Chambers Street, where it still stands above City Hall Park (the Sun Building). The Chambers Street store became Stewart's wholesale outlet. Not only was the new store daringly far uptown, it was probably the largest of all cast-iron buildings and the first with interior cast-iron columns and girders. Designed by architect John Kellum in Italian palazzo style, the five-story exterior, painted white, was majestic with street-level sheets of plate glass between tall Corinthian columns and, above, four tiers of 84 identical arched windows. Inside, the upper floors rose in galleries around a great central rotunda to a huge skylight. Five hundred clerks and cashiers, all male, were employed on the first three floors. On the two top floors, 800 women worked as seamstresses, dressmakers, and in a linen service. Hours were long, but working conditions were among the best in the city.

Each day, the grand staircases and six steam-driven elevators carried as many as 15,000 shoppers, mostly female. Selling all manner of merchandise and services, Stewart's was America's first true department

store. Stewart's conviction that everyone would recognize the store kept the facade free of signs and advertisements and increased the building's distinction.

A.T. Stewert's great store attracted thousands of shoppers each day but Sunday.

Some idea of the prices at A. T. Stewart Company can be gleaned from the shopping adventures of Mrs. Abraham Lincoln, a compulsive buyer who made many trips to Broadway and Tenth Street. Unable to decide between a shawl that cost $650 and another that cost $1,000, she bought both. In *Mary Todd Lincoln: Her Life and Letters,* Justin and Linda Turner write that Mrs. Lincoln confessed to her maid in 1864 that she owed $27,000 in unpaid bills, mostly to A. T. Stewart.[15]

Stewart's Tenth Street store was only part of an empire of hotels, mills, and other businesses that made him the second wealthiest man in the city after John Jacob Astor. Immediately after the Civil War, he ordered up a white marble mansion on the northwest corner of Fifth Avenue and Thirty-Fourth Street that cost $3 million to build and furnish. With broad, sculpture-lined halls, sweeping staircases, an art gallery, and a ballroom, the house set a new standard for extravagance. Stewart was also an open-handed philanthropist and a man with the foresight to develop one of the first planned suburban communities, Garden City, Long Island.

Stewart's fame faded into notoriety after his death in 1876. Body snatchers stole his corpse from the graveyard at St. Mark's in the Bowery and held it for nearly two years before a $20,000 ransom was agreed upon. Not so macabre but more damaging to his reputation and to the survival of his store was the anti-Semitic incident at his Grand Union Hotel in Saratoga in 1877. For many summers, Joseph Seligman, a banking peer of the Rothschilds and Morgans, had vacationed with his family at the Grand Union. As the story is told by Stephen Birmingham in *Our Crowd*, business at the Grand Union had begun to fall off.[16] Apparently Stewart and certainly the executor of his will, Judge Henry Hilton (a member of the Tweed Ring), believed that business had declined because Christian guests did not want to share the glorious hostelry with Jews. Seligman was advised that the Grand Union no longer accepted "Israelites." The refusal erupted into a nationwide headline sensation and led to a massive boycott of Stewart's store. Birmingham writes that the continuing boycott had a good deal to do with the store's eventual failure and sale to John Wanamaker in 1896.

Even before the opening of Stewart's grand emporium, Broadway above Tenth Street had become a center for society and fashion with the building of Grace Church in 1847 and the elegant St. Denis Hotel at Eleventh Street in 1848. Both were architectural triumphs for the young James Renwick Jr. Stewart's immediate success transformed the neighborhood by inspiring many of New York's leading retailers to move uptown to what became known as Ladies' Mile.[17] Lord & Taylor, James McCreery, Rogers Peet, Brooks Brothers, Arnold Constable, F. A. O. Schwartz, W & J Sloane, Crouch & Fitzgerald, Tiffany, Bergdorf Goodman, Arnold Constable, Best's, B. Altman's, Macy's, Reed & Barton, Gorham, Siegal-Cooper, Hugh O'Neil, and others built their own grand edifices or leased shops on the blocks beginning at Tenth Street. This area was the center for the sale of pianos, with Steinway, Chickering, Sohmer, and Knabe among dozens of showrooms for what was then a major New York industry. Ladies Mile turned from Broadway at Union Square, continued across Fourteenth Street to Sixth Avenue, then continued up to Twenty-Third Street. A Broadway branch that resumed at Nineteenth Street cut across Twentieth to Fifth Avenue, then up to Twenty-Third.

Whether a shopper began or ended her tour of the stores at A. T. Stewart, she was likely to stop at Fleishman's Model Vienna Bakery on the northeast corner of Broadway and Tenth Street for coffee or chocolate and pastries.[18] In warm weather, tables were set behind trellises and beneath striped awnings. The midnight scene was something else.

Fleishmann's Vienna Model Bakery, situated between A.T. Stewert and Grace Church, was famed for pastries and free bread given to the homeless at midnight.

As theater crowds headed home, shabbily dressed men—homeless or residents of flophouses—formed an orderly line waiting for free leftovers and coffee. The length of the queue, which could stretch up Broadway for blocks, was a gauge of economic conditions. In 1905, Grace Church purchased the ground on which Fleishman's stood. Three years later, it leveled the building to make way for the green known as Huntington Close, in honor of the church's sixth rector.

Ladies' Mile was more than a place for shopping or social gathering. It was here that New York's preeminence in publishing and design as well as fashion first became apparent. Wealthy New Yorkers and visitors were attracted by its fine restaurants and hotels, concert halls, theaters, and galleries.

The Athenaeum Quarter

By the middle of the nineteenth century, the area around Astor Place and Washington Square was known as the Athenaeum Quarter because of its cluster of libraries, bookstores, art galleries, the Astor Place Opera House, NYU, and the newly opened Cooper Union for the Advancement of Science and Art. Here the seeds were planted for both the Metropolitan Museum of Art and the New York Public Library.

What Philip Hone called the "swellest" house in the city was on University Place between Ninth and Tenth Streets. It belonged to shipping and railroad tycoon William H. Aspinwall, for whom the first New York clipper ship, *Rainbow*, had been built. Part of the mansion was turned into an impressive art gallery, the first in the city that was open to the public. His son-in-law James Renwick Jr. lived across University Place at Tenth in a home that the *New York Times* compared to a museum. John Taylor Johnston, president of the Lehigh and Susquehanna Railroad and the Central of New Jersey Railroad, had built his white marble mansion on the southwest corner of Fifth Avenue and Eighth Street. The second floor of the attached stable was turned into a gallery for his growing collection of art. In 1870, a decision was made at the Union League Club to found a permanent public showplace for art that would include the collections of Johnston, Aspinwall, Renwick, and others. This would become the Metropolitan Museum of Art, with Johnston as its first president. His son-in-law, Robert DeForest became the fifth president. In 1858, John Taylor Johnston's brother James Boorman Johnston had hired Richard Morris Hunt to design the first building devoted entirely to the business of art, the Tenth Street Studios between Fifth and Sixth Avenues. Frederic Church, John LaFarge, Albert Bierstadt, Winslow Homer, and William Merritt Chase set up shop in the studios.

The oldest library in the city, the New York Society Library, founded in 1754 as a private subscription service, moved uptown to University Place in 1856. The New York Mercantile Library, founded in 1820 as a circulating library by merchant clerks, moved to Astor Place in 1854. The Astor Library opened in 1852 on Lafayette Place. It was the city's first public library, free to all, but readers could not borrow from a reference collection that eventually amounted to some 200,000 volumes—mostly literature and American history. A half-dozen blocks away on University Place and Twelfth Street was the mansion of James Lenox, who built a private library around groups of rare books and art objects. In 1895, the Astor and Lenox collections were combined by the trust of Samuel J. Tilden to form a majestic reference and circulating library that would rise on the site of the Croton reservoir at Fifth Avenue and Forty-Second Street.

Booksellers' Row began a couple of blocks below the Astor Library at DeVinne Press—publisher of the *Century Dictionary*, the *Book of Common Prayer*, other scholarly works, and *Scribners'*, *Century*, and *St. Nicholas* magazines—and ran to Brentano's Literary Emporium on Union Square. Bible House, the world's largest publisher of religious tracts, several fashionable bookstores, and nearly 20 used bookstores were neighbors of Sailors' Snug Harbor at Astor Place and along Fourth Avenue.

During the 1840s and 1850s, the center of New York's literary world was located in the comfortable basement of the townhouse at 10 Eighth Street, just east of Fifth Avenue. This was home and workplace of Evert A. Duyckinck, a gentlemanly scholar who served as advisor to countless writers and literary tradesmen including Herman Melville, Nathaniel Hawthorne, Washington Irving, and William Cullen Bryant.[19] Each week, over punch and cigars, they indulged in the best of literary conversation and borrowed from his library of 18,000 books. Duyckinck was editor of the brilliant *Literary World* and, with his brother George, compiled the 10-pound, two-volume *Cyclopaedia of American Literature*, a standard reference work to this day.

Thirty years later, the leading artists and writers of the day gathered across Eighth Street at number 13, home of Richard Watson Gilder, another hospitable and influential editor who had made *Century* America's most prestigious journal.

NYU's University Building was a major contributor to the area's erudite atmosphere, in part because it had to rent space to balance its budget. Among the tenants were the New-York Historical Society; the American Institute of Architects; the New York Academy of Medicine; the American Geographical Society; and Samuel F. B. Morse, who took a half-dozen rooms as studios for his students and himself. Well known as an artist, Morse was also professor of painting and sculpture at the university; first president and a founder of the National Academy of Design, which had exhibition galleries at Tenth Street and Fourth Avenue; and a member of the Century Club, where wealthy merchants paid social homage to the city's leading artists and writers at their meeting rooms on Eighth and Greene Streets. Morse, gradually abandoning art for science, experimented in his NYU laboratory for a dozen years to perfect the electric

This pen-ink-wash drawing is one of the earliest pictures of New Yorkers at play, including two cats on the roof. Inscribed Serenade 12 January 1841, it is from an album of sketches by an unknown artist. The address, 823 Broadway, would have been on the newly developed Brevoort farm a bit north of Tenth Street.

Peter Cooper and Cooper Union, which offered the city's only "Free Reading Room for Males and Females." The walls carried mercantile ads because for the school's first 40 years it had to rent out its first, second, and top floors.

telegraph. He demonstrated its practicality to Congress in 1844 by transmitting messages by wire from Baltimore to Washington, D.C. Morse collaborated with fellow professor John W. Draper on the development of the daguerreotype. Draper took the first sunlit photo of the human face on the roof of the University Building in 1840. Samuel Colt worked on the design of his revolver while living in the South Tower. Among the 67 artists who resided in the University Building between 1834 and 1894 were Eastman Johnson, Winslow Homer, George Inness, and Anna Mary Freeman, the lone woman.

Cooper Union, founded in 1859 by inventor-manufacturer Peter Cooper at Astor Place, provided free courses in practical subjects, including art and engineering, for working people of all creeds and races. Beneath his high-rise brownstone, Cooper built the Great Hall where he expected the important issues of the day to be discussed. Within the year, Abraham Lincoln delivered his "Might Makes Right" speech from the stage of the Great Hall to a highly impressed audience of New York editors and Republican leaders. Earlier in the day he had his photograph taken by Matthew Brady, who came to fame with his pictorial portrayal of the Civil War. The widely distributed speech and photo introduced the little-known Illinois politician to Americans everywhere. Legend has Lincoln crediting Cooper Union and Brady with winning the White House for him. A few weeks after taking

Lincoln's photograph, Brady moved from a studio below Bleecker Street to a splendid second-floor gallery above Daniel & Son, purveyor of ladies garments across Broadway from A. T. Stewart on the southwest corner of Tenth Street.

Houses of worship are an integral element in any neighborhood aspiring to be an Athenaeum Quarter. The Washington Square neighborhood had a fair share of the churches that followed their congregations uptown, beginning with the South Dutch Reformed in 1840. The Church of the Ascension, low Episcopal, was completed on Fifth Avenue at Tenth Street in 1841 by Richard Upjohn, a busy architect. His Trinity Church would open at the head of Wall Street in 1843, and his University Place Presbyterian (at Tenth Street) held its first services in 1844. Architect James C. Wells's First Presbyterian, at Fifth Avenue and Twelfth Street, dates to 1846. Both the downtown originals of Ascension and First Presbyterian were destroyed by fires. Grace Episcopal was so much the church of the social elite that, when it opened in 1846, it was said to have made its debut. St. Ann's Roman Catholic Church was completed in the late 1840s on Eighth Street near Fourth Avenue. The Church of the Strangers, a Presbyterian parish on Mercer Street between Waverly Place and Eighth, was built in 1835. Parishioners were joined at Sunday services by many travelers from nearby hotels. Union Theological Seminary, a graduate school for Protestant ministers, opened on University Place near Eighth Street in 1836. The seminary and the Church of the Strangers were located on Harbor property. All of the churches except St. Ann's were Gothic Revival in style.

A Parisian Touch: Red Lights and Riots

In his *Incredible New York*, Lloyd Morris writes that in 1850 "New York seemed a city of crowds and carnival—breezy, recklessly extravagant, perpetually bent on pleasure. The bright gaslights of bars and restaurants and hotels threw a glare over Broadway until well toward dawn."

Immediately to the west of Broadway are Mercer, Greene, and Wooster, then quiet-looking streets of red-brick houses that shared, in their own disreputable way, in all the excitement. In the 1850s, there were at least 30 houses of prostitution on Mercer and 15 each on Greene and Wooster in the half-dozen blocks between Canal and Bleecker. The gas lamps that glowed in bowls of red-tinted glass above the brothel doors had been moving steadily north toward the boundaries of Sailors' Snug Harbor. The trustees and their tenants, however,

Streetwalkers in the neighborhood of Mercer, Green, and Wooster Streets, site of 30 or more brothels in pre–Civil War days and nights.

were saved from whatever embarrassment such neighbors might bring when the red-light district shifted in the years immediately after the Civil War to the Tenderloin, the blocks above Twenty-Third Street between Sixth and Eighth Avenues.[20] Actually, one bordello did find its way onto Harbor property on Eighth Street between University Place and Broadway, but it was extraordinarily discreet and exclusive. The proprietor Josie Woods drew her clientele from New York's aristocracy, and even those gentlemen were required to provide preliminary certification before an initial visit.

Astor Place: Opera Tragique

New York's eminent citizenry expected the Astor Place Opera House to bestow upon them classical music, high drama, and good humor when it opened in 1847 immediately next to property owned by Sailors' Snug Harbor.[21] The traditional open seating of the pit had become a reserved-seat parquet, surrounded on three sides by two tiers of splendid subscription boxes. Above was a nonreserved gallery, where the view from hard seats was partially blocked by a chandelier. Gentlemen observed a dress code calculated to discourage the middle class and working classes—freshly shaven face, silk vest, and kid gloves.

In their expectations, the gentry had not taken into account the flamboyance and volatile temper of Edwin Forrest, who considered himself the greatest tragedian of the day (although a more accurate characterization may have been supplied by the critic who described him "as a vast animal bewildered by a grain of genius"). During a recent visit to Britain, Forrest had publicly disparaged the Hamlet of the aristocratic Englishman William Charles Macready, who disdained any hint of vulgarity. Macready's partisans, however, took to humiliating Forrest each time he stepped on stage. This led to an exchange of unpleasantness in the British and American press.

Soon after, Macready and company embarked on an American tour that was to conclude at Astor Place. When the Englishman opened as Macbeth on May 7, 1849, he was greeted with hissing, shouts, rotten eggs, and other missiles by supporters of Forrest. Captain Isaiah Rynders, Tammany boss of the notorious Sixth Ward, and his nativist cohort, dime novelist Ned Bundline, had salted the house with scores of "Bowery boys," working-class brawlers who remembered Forrest fondly from his days as a star at the Bowery Theater.

A frustrated Macready was packing for London when presented with a petition from 47 leading citizens, including Washington Irving and Herman Melville, urging him to continue his engagement. They promised their support and that of the general public and the police. Macready agreed to return to the stage as Macbeth on Thursday evening, May 10.

A roaring crowd of 10,000 to 15,000 appeared in Astor Place to shout him down again. No festering tiff between thin-skinned actors— even when fed by the likes of Rynders—could account for a turnout of this size. Clearly Macready symbolized aristocracy to this Anglophobic crowd made up of workingmen inspired by the revolutions that had convulsed Europe in 1848 and of Irishmen driven from their homeland by famine and still another failed rebellion.

Unarmed police were unable to stop the showers of paving blocks and bricks that smashed the Opera House windows. Eventually, Seventh Regiment troops, quartered in an armory on the site of what is now Cooper Union's Hewitt Building, opened fire. Twenty-two were killed and an estimated150 wounded. A dozen of the dead had Irish names including Bridgit Fagan, shot while walking with her husband. None were Bowery boys.

Postmortems indicated that only a small portion of the crowd—as few as 500, mostly teenagers—had actually assaulted the building. Although Forrest's followers were cited as instigators, the riot was found to be directed mainly at the Opera House itself as an ostentatious affront to traditional republican notions of simplicity.

Macready fled to England, never to return. Forrest, more popular than ever, went on to amass a fortune. The Opera House, barely three years old, was closed in 1850 and refitted as Clinton Hall by the Mercantile Library. It was demolished in 1890. For many years in the latter half of the twentieth century, the still-existing office-building replacement served as headquarters of District 50, the catchall segment of the United Mine Workers.

New Yorkers had been primed for a disaster such as that in Astor Place since mobs of colonists demonstrated successfully against the Stamp Act in 1765. Rioting had become commonplace. For two days in

Riot at the Astor Place Opera House, May 10, 1849: Macbeth and Death.

April 1788, 5,000 citizens, suspecting that medical students were stealing cadavers from cemeteries, ransacked New York Hospital. In 1806, Catholics and Protestants battled on Christmas Day. Stevedores, weavers, and stonecutters struck violently during the 1820s. As the Civil War approached, abolitionists and their foes fought a series of street battles. Bloodiest of all were the turf duels between gangs in the Bowery and their Five-Point neighbors. Twelve died in one July 4 test of strength.

Upper- and middle-class fears of continued social unrest led to the construction of 29 regimental armories in the city in the years following the Civil War. Greenwich Village came under the protective arms of the Ninth Regiment, which set up headquarters on Fourteenth Street.

The Civil War

President Lincoln answered South Carolina's shelling of Fort Sumter on April 12, 1861, with a call for 75,000 volunteers. Within weeks, more than 8,000 New Yorkers were in uniform including a regiment with headquarters on University Place and Thirteenth Street. According to the plaque on the building that now stands at 115 University Place, "The 83rd New York Volunteers . . . marched away 850 strong on May 27, 1861." As the Ninth Regiment, they joined the Army of the Potomac and fought in 28 battles—Bull Run, Antietam, Chancellorsville, Gettysburg, and the Wilderness among them. Two months after General Robert E. Lee surrendered at Appomattox, the 95 heroic survivors of the 83rd Volunteers returned home. In three years of war, 755 members of their regiment had fallen.

The Draft Riots

Victories at Vicksburg and Gettysburg would turn the Civil War around within three months, but in spring 1863 the fortunes of the Union Army appeared so low that Congress passed a conscription bill making all men between the ages of 20 and 45 liable for military service. All men, that is, who could not afford to purchase $300 exemptions. Members of the working class—and that meant Irish immigrants, for the most part—were insulted by the waiver. Tammany's "Copperhead" Democrats, favoring peace even at the price of southern separation, had already been fanning class anger by warning that Irish jobs were endangered by Lincoln's Emancipation Proclamation.

The draft lottery began as scheduled at the provost marshal's office at Third Avenue and Forty-Seventh Street on Monday morning July 13. Mobs of workingmen, bricks and clubs at the ready, forced the provost marshall to flee and burned the building. That was the beginning of the bloodiest riot in American history. Thousands of rioters—estimates run as high as 50,000—controlled much of the city for the better part of four days and nights.[22]

Shops and homes of Republican leaders and abolitionists were sacked, telegraph lines cut, tracks torn up, and factories forced to close. Policemen—nearly all of them Irish—and African Americans were special targets. Superintendent of Police John A. Kennedy, out of uniform but recognized by the rioters, was stabbed and beaten until nearly dead. The Colored Orphan Asylum was torched minutes after the last of 200 children were shepherded out a rear entrance. Eleven blacks were murdered, including five hanged from lampposts and tree limbs. For the most part, rioters confined themselves to uptown districts and the waterfront. Revenge was a factor in the dock area because, a month earlier, freed slaves, guarded by Federal troops, had broken a longshoremen's strike.

One major battle was fought in the vicinity of Washington Square at Broadway and Third Street. A mob intent upon destroying police headquarters at 300 Mulberry Street was intercepted in its downtown march by 125 policemen and scores of volunteers. The marchers were dispersed after 30 minutes of hand-to-hand combat. Astor Place served as a marshaling ground for downtown combatants preparing to join the uptown melee. Only in Greenwich Village did some black families dare to take up arms to protect their persons and property.

Estimates of the death toll ran as high as 2,000. Iver Bernstein's authoritative 1990 study of the riots concludes that "at least 105 died"—

nearly five times more than the Astor Place fatalities. The number of wounded remains countless. Some 300 buildings were destroyed by fire or damaged and looted.

Many Republicans and some Democrats were convinced that the riots were part of a Confederate conspiracy to coordinate southern military victories with a mob takeover of New York. A federal investigation found no evidence of a planned uprising. Bernstein, who discounts the conspiracy theories, notes, "It is fair to speculate . . . that if Confederate General Robert E. Lee had pushed north from Gettysburg at the moment rioting erupted in New York City, European intervention would have stalemated the war." As it happened, on that first night of the riots Lee crossed the Potomac in his retreat to the south.

The Plot to Burn New York

Some 16 months later, on November 25, 1864, a cabal of Confederate officers and Copperheads, or Peace Democrats, attempted to destroy New York as part of a conspiracy to take control of the city.[23] The conspiracy was inspired by the desperate Jefferson Davis in spring 1864, when he commissioned Confederate Army Colonel Jacob Thompson to find a way of bringing the Copperheads into the war. With a budget of $300,000, Thompson—former Mississippi congressman, member of President James Buchanan's cabinet, and aide to Confederate General P. G. T. Beauregard—set up in the Queen's Hotel in Toronto, a neutral site and wartime refuge of hundreds of southerners, spies, informers, and New York City detectives who visited occasionally to keep an eye on the situation. Contact with Richmond was entrusted to couriers who carried forged papers back and forth through the United States. At least one courier was a spy for the North. Whether the result of undercover work or his staff's incompetence, Thompson's schemes to foment rebellion in the North had failed.

Finally, an editorial from a Richmond newspaper that was reprinted in the *New York Times* may have inspired an exploit that seriously threatened Manhattan. Reporting that Union Army General Philip Sheridan had burned 2,000 barns and 70 mills in the Shenandoah Valley, the editorial proclaimed that the only way to stop such atrocity "is to burn one of the chief cities of the enemy."

Thompson targeted New York. A team of eight Confederate officers under the command of Colonel Robert M. Martin, a wounded survivor of the famous Morgan Raiders, was mobilized. Second in command was another Morgan officer, Lieutenant John W. Headley. Wearing civilian clothes and using fictitious names, the rebels traveled by train from Toronto to New York on October 26, 13 days before the time set for their attack, November 8, election day. War weariness and Lincoln's insistence on the abolition of slavery made his Democratic opponent for the presidency, General George B. McClellan, confident of victory. Unlike many Copperheads, McClellan believed that the Confederates had to be defeated but he promised he would restore the Union as it existed before the war and emancipation.

Each southern officer was assigned multiple targets to douse with "Greek fire," a bottled mixture of turpentine and phosphorus that burst into flame when exposed to air. If all went as planned, the diversionary fires and the traffic jams they caused would clear the way for Copperhead seizures of federal and municipal offices, including the police department and Fort Lafayette, a prison for Confederate officers in New York harbor.

On arrival in New York, Martin, Headley and Captain Robert Cobb Kennedy, a recent escapee from military prison in Ohio, had checked into the luxurious St. Denis at Eleventh Street and Broadway. (Presumably, they did not know that this was Mrs. Abraham Lincoln's favorite hotel because of its proximity to A. T. Stewart's department store.) On Friday morning, October 28, the Confederate trio met at the office of their liaison, James A. McMaster, publisher of the *Freeman's Journal*. McMaster and the eight soldiers, who had begun moving individually from hotel to hotel to avoid detection, held a series of planning sessions. The traitorous New Yorker assured the officers that he had 20,000 men, mostly armed, awaiting his call. What none of the conspirators knew was that the War Department and the New York police were aware of the plot. On November 4, Union General Benjamin Butler arrived in New York with 3,500 troops—rumored to be 15,000—and cast a military cordon around the city. Election day passed without incident.

Lincoln lost by a two-to-one margin in 21 of New York City's 22 wards. The Fifteenth Ward—which included Sailors' Snug Harbor and its neighbors from Broadway to Sixth Avenue, Houston to Fourteenth Street—favored Lincoln over McClellan, 2,224 to 1,940. The president carried the state and the electoral college by 212 to 21.[24]

Copperhead will collapsed and could not be revived, even with the return of Butler and his troops to the battlefront on November 15. Six of the Confederate band stayed in the city, determined to make a payback for the suffering South. In a borrowed cottage in the city's new Central Park, they developed a new plan. Because of guards, no public buildings would be attacked. Each would book rooms in two or more of the city's best hotels and, at the appointed time, bundle linen, chairs, bureau drawers, and drapes on the bed and torch the pile with Greek fire.

The grand conflagration was scheduled to begin on the evening of November 25, a special New York holiday celebrating the evacuation of British troops in 1783. The first alarm, from the St. James Hotel, at Broadway near Madison Square, sounded at 8:43 P.M.

Within minutes, fires were reported at the St. Nicholas (on Broadway at Spring Street) and LaFarge House (at Broadway and Bond Street). Tolling from the watch towers continued through dawn. The final alarm, nearly 12 hours after the first, reported a fire at the Astor House, across Broadway from St. Paul's Church. The arsonists struck 13 hotels, Barnum's Museum, and a pier and barge on the Hudson River. False alarms caused audiences to stampede at Niblo's Garden and the Winter Garden Theater. Somehow, no one was seriously hurt and only one of the hotels, the St. Nicholas, was badly damaged. Volunteer firemen—usually noted more for brawling than firefighting—and hotel employees quickly brought the fires under control.

There was more than good work in all this. After studying the burnt sites, Fire Marshal Alfred Baker reported that in each case doors and windows were left closed; when the phosphorus ignited, it only smoldered because of a lack of oxygen. This slight miscalculation defeated the southerners, he concluded.

The disappointed guerrillas were back in Toronto by Monday afternoon. New York detectives arrived soon after with descriptions of four suspects including Robert Kennedy, who walked with a distinctive limp caused by a wound suffered at the battle of Shiloh. Hoping to return to his old outfit, Kennedy obtained a false passport, a pass to get through Southern lines, and a $20 Confederate bill from Thompson. The latter two items were sewn into a jacket sleeve. On December 28, two detectives spotted Kennedy buying a railroad ticket to Detroit and they wired an alert.

Kennedy was arrested outside the Detroit depot that evening by two other New York detectives. The 29-year-old captain from Louisiana was taken to New York under guard, and tried by a six-member military commission on charges of spying and attempting to set New York afire. He was found guilty and hanged at Fort Lafayette on March 25, 1865, without identifying any of his fellow arsonists. Lee surrendered 15 days later. Kennedy was the last Confederate soldier executed by the Union.

Martin and Headley were arrested shortly after the war ended. Martin was tried for arson in a civil court, but the charge was dismissed for lack of evidence. Both Martin and Headley received presidential pardons.

Notes

1. For city hall's brownstone, see Edward Robb Ellis, *The Epic of New York City*, p. 197.

2. Anthony Bailey's study of the 1811 grid plan was published by *American Heritage* in a special 1968 issue devoted to the city of New York.

3. Volume 1, 1815, of the "General Shipping List, New York," published every Tuesday and Friday, tracks the arrivals and departures in a suddenly busy harbor. This is available in the library of the South Street Seaport Museum.

4. For Albany's auction legislation, see Robert G. Albion, *The Rise of the Port of New York: 1815-1860*, p. 13. On the same page, Albion warns against oversimplifying the explanation of the port's rise by attributing everything to the opening of the Erie Canal.

5. The opening pages of John Malcolm Brinnin's *The Sway of the Grand Saloon* carry a colorful account of the launching of the Black Ball Line on a winter's morning from Pier 23 on South Street.

6. Hone's quotes are from his *Diary* (1:203), edited by Bayard Tuckerman.

7. The *Evening Post* hanging report appears in Edmund Delaney's *New York's Greenwich Village*, p. 52.

8. In a letter to the *New York Times* on August 8, 1994, Luther Harris, a Washington Square historian, explained why the hanging-tree story is all myth.

9. On St. John's Park, see Charles Lockwood, *Manhattan Moves Uptown*, p. 7.

10. Excerpts from the first chapter of Luther Harris's history of Washington Square appeared in the spring 1999 edition of *Seaport*, the quarterly magazine of the South Street Seaport Museum.

11. The *Greenwich Village Historical District Designation Report*, 1969, vol. 1, was particularly helpful in writing this section. It was published by the Landmarks Preservation Commission. Among the

books that added to my knowledge of time and place were Bayard Still's *Mirror for Gotham* and his description in *Greenwich Village: Culture and Counterculture* (edited by Rick Beard and Leslie Cohen Berlowitz) of the Washington Square neighborhood in the mid-nineteenth century; Charles Lockwood's *Manhattan Moves Uptown*; and Terry Miller's *Greenwich Village and How It Got That Way*.

12. Stern's report on the remodeling appears in *New York 1900*, p. 383.

13. Professor Landau's question about the leftover brick appears in Rick Beard and Leslie Cohen Berlowitz, eds., *Greenwich Village: Culture and Counterculture*, p. 70.

14. Reminiscences, *New York Times*, May 12, 1938.

15. See *Mary Todd Lincoln: Her Life and Letters*, ed. Justin G. Turner and Linda Levitt Turner, pp. 88, 163.

16. Stephen Birmingham, *Our Crowd*, pp. 141–3.

17. Margaret Moore and the Municipal Art Society record its history in *End of the Road for Ladies' Mile?*

18. Grace Mayer's *Once Upon a City* contains a delightful photograph of Fleishman's Model Vienna Bakery, p. 10.

19. Duycknick's salon is described in *Literary History of the United States*, p. 240.

20. Timothy J. Gilfoyle tells the red-light story in *City of Eros: New York City Prostitution and the Commercialization of Sex, 1790–1920*. For a report on Madam Wood's classy bordello, see Lloyd Morris, *Incredible New York*, p. 47.

21. John F. Kasson includes the Astor Place riots in his *Rudeness and Civility: Manners in Nineteenth-Century Urban America*, pp. 222–9.

22. The definitive account of *The New York City Draft Riots* was written in 1990 by Iver Bernstein. The death toll estimate appears on page 5.

23. In *The Epic of New York City*, Edward Robb Ellis includes accounts of the draft riots and the plot to burn the city. Nat Brandt's *The Man Who Tried to Burn New York* adds details about the plot and the plotters.

24. Lincoln's victory over McClellan in the Fifteenth Ward was reported on the front page of the *New York Tribune*, November 9, 1864.

Why Men Go Down to the Sea

Admitting an aged and worn out sailor to the Harbor.

ovelist Theodore Dreiser lived in the immediate vicinity of Sailors' Snug Harbor on Staten Island for nearly a year in the early 1920s. The author of *An American Tragedy* visited the old sailors on the grounds of their retreat and chatted with them in the few saloons of the region as well as the coffeehouses, small lunch counters, and moving picture theaters. Although he was impressed with the beauty of the Harbor's buildings and grounds, Dreiser found many of the old seamen restless and remorseful. He was convinced that most of them would be happier if set free with a modest pension, a theme to recur in the Harbor's future. His impressions of the Harbor and its tenants were included in *The Color of a Great City*, a collection of New York scenes published in 1923.[1]

One of his favorite tales came from a seaman who had rounded the dangerous Cape Horn 49 times in a sailing vessel. "Will you tell me an adventure of the sea?" Dreiser asked. The seaman answered:

I could, but I would rather tell you of thirteen peaceful years here. I came here when I was seventy, though at sixty, when I was weathering a terrible storm around the Cape with little hope of ever seeing the rising sun, I promised myself that if I reached home again I would stay there. But I didn't know myself even then. My destiny was to remain on the sea for ten years more, with this Harbor for my few remaining years. At that, if I were young I would go to sea again, I believe. It's the only life for me.

A somewhat different answer came from another old salt when asked if he would return to the sea if he were young again. "Not I," came the reply. "If I were to sail four thousand times I'd be as seasick the last trip as on the first day out. Every blessed trip I made for the first five years I nearly died of seasickness."

"Why did you keep it up then?" Dreiser asked. "Well, when I'd get to port everybody would ask: 'How did you like it? Are you going again?' 'Of course I am,' I would answer. And then I went from pure shamefacedness and not to be outdone. After a while I didn't mind it so much, and finally I kept to it 'cause I couldn't do anything else."

"The here and the now. That's it." James C. Healey, a seaman himself before he became a chaplain in the port of New York, found that a sailor's wants are generally immediate—a bed; a meal; cigarettes; a pair of dungarees; bus fare to Boston or Baltimore; a letter to a port captain, a social worker, or a legal-aid lawyer. "These help to meet 90 percent of the average seaman's needs," he wrote in *Foc's'le and Glory Hole*, his 1936 study of merchant sailors. "The plans for a week or a month hence are beautifully vague. Tomorrow will always take care of itself."[2]

And then there were sailors like Howard Flynn, who first went to sea as a youngster on his father's schooner along with his mother and three brothers for a trading trip from Maine to the West Indies and back. All four of the boys earned their master's license. Flynn told the *New York Herald-Tribune* in the 1930s, "The days on the old sailing vessels passed very quickly. There was always something to do, never time to loaf. I never missed anything I could have had on land. A seaman usually feels happy to get away from the troubles in port." After he became master of a coastal schooner, his wife sailed with him most of the time. Flynn was elected governor of Sailors' Snug Harbor in 1935.[3]

While living at the Harbor in the 1920s, Captain William Morris

Barnes wrote his reminiscences in a slender book called *When Ships Were Ships and Not Tin Pots*. He was another who would have gone back to sea. He wrote:

> What I liked about it most is that it's not humdrum—not monotonous—there's always some excitement—something to look forward to—there's a gale coming and you're expecting to see some sea come and do damage—it's all the time changing, see, from one day to the other, from one month to the other . . . you go to a port tomorrow that you have never been to before. Now on shore, there's one darn thing all the time. A man sits down to his work and if he's a carpenter he's working over and over and over again—the plane and the chisel—aw, it's slow and there's no excitement in it.

With more of a literary touch, Ishmael, Herman Melville's young deckhand and narrator in *Moby Dick*, spoke about his lack of interest in shore life.

> Whenever it is a damp, drizzly November in my soul, . . . I quietly take to the ship. There is nothing surprising in this. If they but knew it, almost all men in their degree, some time or other, cherish very nearly the same feelings towards the ocean with me. Circumambulate the city of a dreamy Sabbath afternoon. . . . What do you see?—Posted like silent sentinels all around the town, stand thousands upon thousands of mortal men fixed in ocean reveries. These are all landsmen; of week days pent up in lath and plaster—tied to counters, nailed to benches, clinched to desks.[4]

In *Two Years before the Mast*, Richard Henry Dana Jr. explained simply, "There is a witchery in the sea."[5]

Captain Samuel Samuels—who took "French leave" of home at age 11 to discover new lands, encounter pirates, capture slavers, rescue a Christian damsel from a Turkish harem, and command the great Atlantic clipper *Dreadnought*—wrote an autobiography called *From the Forecastle to the Cabin*, in which he warns, "The rough experience I have gone through, few could live to endure. I have seen many a man who started with me in this race of a daring and reckless life fall early in the journey." His book makes it clear that he would not hesitate to do it all over again.[6]

Packet-ship captains, who normally retired as rich men, were exceptions to an unwritten but oft-spoken rule of the sea that when age, injury, or circumstance overtook the average free-spending sailor he ended up ashore with empty pockets. The fortunate among these seamen found their way to Randall's Snug Harbor on Staten Island.

Meeting the Residents

By 1850, the Harbor's rural mixture of land and sea was home to nearly 300 retired mariners. Almost a third of them were foreigners who had spent at least 10 years at sea, 5 of those on vessels flying the Stars and Stripes. Dana, when he became a deckhand in the 1830s, claimed that more than three-quarters of the crews on American merchant ships hailed from Britain, Northern Europe, or countries bordering the Mediterranean.[7] The great maritime historian Samuel Eliot Morison, writing about the same years, suggests that 20 percent might be closer to the mark. In either case, why so many non-Americans? According to Morison, "The European type of sailor . . . content to serve before the mast his whole lifetime," was almost unknown in New England. The wanderlust of young men, lured to sea by adventure and good wages, was quickly cured for most by the hard and dangerous life. Those who made the sea their calling aspired to the officers' deck or became "victims of drink" who had no recourse but to ship out again and again. Morison's observations about sailors from New England were applicable to sailors from the Mid-Atlantic states as well, although to a lesser degree because the ports of New York and Philadelphia had far larger back-country populations from which to draw a "deep-sea proletariat."[8]

Morison's view that few Yankees willingly chose a career as a deckhand overlooked a special segment of the population, free blacks. Seafaring offered African Americans mobility and economic opportunity, and many signed on for what they hoped would be a lifetime, no matter the hardships. In *Black Jacks: African American Seamen in the Age of Sail*, W. Jeffrey Bolster reports that early in the nineteenth century America's fast-expanding maritime trade employed more than 100,000 men a year. In 1836, blacks made up 30 percent of the crews sailing from Providence and 14 percent of those shipping out of New York. After the Civil War, opportunities ebbed and racial discrimination intensified as jobs began to disappear in a shrinking merchant service. By 1866, blacks

filled only 5 percent of the berths shipping out of New York.[9]

Although a large number of these black jacks may have retired at Sailors' Snug Harbor, it is not possible to say how many actually became snugs. From the beginning, the Harbor, after checking eligibility, recorded only date and place of birth, never race or religion. Studio portraits of new retirees were made for 20 years near the beginning of the twentieth century. A recent survey of the old photo albums found that only about 30 of the hundreds of men in the pictures appeared to be African American. Had photos been taken a couple of decades earlier, when the population of elderly black seamen was much larger, the number of African American faces in the albums might have been higher. We do know that on September 6, 1842, William Watson became the first black sailor admitted to the Harbor.

Wherever they hailed from originally, these men had sailed in every sea. They spoke with familiarity of East India, China, and the Antarctic. Many had distinguished battle records. We do not know if any snug sailed in the navy of John Barry and John Paul Jones; the Revolution ended 50 years before the opening of the Harbor. But seamen who served in the War of 1812 and all the wars that followed were well represented in the ranks of the Harbor's mariners. Cornelius Rose, according to his official papers, served 35 years in the U.S. Navy, 9 of them aboard the *Constitution*, and took part in 27 engagements beginning in the War of 1812 and continuing through the Mexican War. James Spencer manned a gun on the frigate *Essex* in its losing battle

Seven old salts enjoy a spring day in 1898.

with two English cruisers in the harbor at Valparaiso in March 1812. Of his shipmates, 89 were killed. Two famed Civil War admirals, David Porter and David Farragut, were captain and midshipman on the *Essex* that day. But none of the old sailors had served under a grander commander than did the Italian-born Captain Devoe. Before coming to the United States, Devoe had served in Napoleon Bonaparte's French Imperial Navy. In the 1880s, as the Harbor population approached 900, the trustees had to limit admissions for a time because so many Civil War veterans were coming aboard—all with war stories to tell. But battles are hardly the only tests of courage at sea.

William Hudson was skipper of the Pacific Mail Steamship Line's *Golden Gate* when it caught fire off the coast of Mexico. He managed to beach the vessel just before it sank, a feat of seamanship that saved the lives of passengers and crew. Benjamin Gardiner commanded the lightship at the Vineyard Sound's notorious *Cross Rip* for many years. Two ships sank under him in gales, but he could report each time "all hands safe." Once in a heavy fog, a full-rigged brig struck what would have been a glancing blow if its bow had not torn into the lightship's pantry. Gardiner, describing the incident, sings out to the other captain, "'What are you a-trying to do?' 'I'm a-trying to find the *Cross Rip*,' says he. 'Well, you found it now, and my pantry, too. Just keep going for you ain't got no business in there.'" When Gardiner told such stories, he became indignant with what he described as "the ignorance exhibited by passing skippers about the position of their vessels."

John M'Ewen had a different, sadder, story. For many years, he was a prominent and successful master of ships in the East India trade. Then he lost his sight, and his profession, and sought refuge at the Harbor. Well into the twentieth century, nearly 20 percent of the residents at any one time were captains who had come upon hard times.

It can be assumed that many of the fantastic chronicles swapped by these world travelers were true, or virtually so. Take, for example, this tale told in the 1930s by John Elofson, a Swede who shipped out of Hamburg in 1887 as a seaman on a 300-ton barkentine headed for West Africa with a cargo of blasting powder and gin, under an ill-tempered skipper named Erikson. While anchoring at Port Suguro, the captain took offense at something Elofson said and rushed at him with fists flying. Our hero ducked under the fists, got behind his attacker, and grabbed his scarf. Unable to breathe, the captain slumped unconscious to the deck. In a minute or two he recovered and quickly hoisted signal flags reporting a mutiny. The armed police detachment that answered the cry for help thought it might be a joke when told that only one of the 11-man crew was a mutineer. Nevertheless, Elofson was taken ashore to stand trial before the German counsel, who sentenced him to what turned out to be eight days of shore leave. He was turned over to the little kingdom's European-educated crown prince for safekeeping. Elofson was assigned a body servant, then taken on a hunting trip by the prince. By the time he returned to the ship, he had gained 10 or 15 pounds. Presumably, this was more than the captain could stand, for he became ill and died on the trip home.

An even longer stretch of maritime memory was tested in 1981 when the square-rigger *Wavertree* became part of the historic fleet at the South Street Seaport Museum in lower Manhattan. James E. Roberts, then in his 90s, crossed the harbor on the Staten Island ferry to visit the ship on which he and fellow teenager George Robinson embarked in 1897 for careers at sea. Roberts would become a ship's master. Robinson, helping to furl an upper topsail in a gale, fell from aloft over the *Wavertree's* side and was lost.[10]

A Visit to the Harbor

Visitors passed through an impressively formal Victorian gatehouse overlooking Richmond Terrace and the Kill Van Kull. The gatekeeper called a guide—one of the resident seamen—who paged the visitors' friend or conducted the uninitiated on a tour of the spacious grounds and elegant buildings, which form a college-like campus. In fair weather, the old seamen—dressed in loose-fitting blue suits from Brooks Brothers with gold buttons and slouch hats—could be seen strolling along well-kept paths, relaxing under the great elms, or sitting on benches smoking pipes and chatting. No one had to get wet or chilled in poor weather because dormitories, dining rooms, and lounges were all connected with enclosed bridges—the architectural hyphens of Minard Lafever. Cribbage, pinochle, and billiards were constants in the recreation rooms. A reading room with a timely collection of international newspapers was a favorite retreat in the large library. Nearly all dormitory chores were handled by matrons, who also oversaw laundry and sewing departments. Most of the able-bodied residents kept busy with hobbies or part-time jobs, and they were rarely required to do any work beyond making their beds and keeping their rooms in order. They were allowed to come and go at will, giving notice at the gate as

*Main entrance to the
Harbor, through the
Italianate gatehouse with
cupola built in 1874.*

would be expected of a member of any family. Visits "ashore" might last for weeks. A fair proportion of the population lived with family or friends at any one time.

Officially, days began with breakfast at seven o'clock, but a majority of the men may have been up for two hours by then; as aboard good ships, coffee hours started at 5 A.M., 9:30, and 2:30. Dinner was at noon, supper at six o'clock. Food, plentiful and varied, was served family style at long tables in four attractive dining halls. Linens were changed three times weekly. Grace was said before and after each meal. A large kitchen, employing a staff of 30, was said to serve up to 1,000 sailors with less noise and confusion than an ordinary housewife makes in cooking for a small family. Here is a typical bill of fare from November 1951: break-fast—stewed fruit, French toast with syrup or jam, soft-boiled eggs, corn flakes with milk, coffee; dinner—vegetable soup, stuffed breast of veal with tomato sauce, steamed rice, boiled potatoes, baked apples, coffee; supper—New England clam chowder, sardines, green peppers stuffed with corn, doughnuts, tea. Dinner entrees from the same week included roast shoulder of pork, liver and sausage links, baked fresh fish, baked Virginia ham, boiled salt codfish or roast mutton, and curried veal.

A few years earlier, the New York State Department of Welfare com-plained that the Harbor's menus were poorly balanced, too starchy, and excessively high in calories. In response, Harbor staff pointed out that the aim of the trustees and administration, with guidance from a pro-fessional dietician, was to serve the mariners foods that they preferred and had become accustomed to during their active lives. Apples and oranges were left untouched on the tables, and the men refused to eat salads of raw vegetables, except for an occasional serving of cole slaw. As to the menus' relation to the life and health of the men, Harbor staff noted that the average age of mariners admitted during the past five years was 71, and the average length of residence of those who died during that period was eight years and seven months. No reply from the welfare department can be found in Harbor records.

The hospital, located at the edge of the Harbor farmlands, stood apart from other buildings, but in size and style it resembled the famous Greek Revival row. In 1901, when an imposing sanitarium with four wings extending from a massive rotunda opened next to and connect-ed with the hospital, the medical center could accommodate 185 patients in nine wards. Of the Harbor's population of 950 at this time, 150 were hospitalized. The expanded facility had its own chapel

The stylish seven-foot fence enclosed 20 of the Harbor's 80 acres.

and dining halls, including one designed for seamen confined to wheel-chairs. A ward was set aside for mentally ill residents who were considered harmless. Violent patients went to state institutions. Residents received dental fixtures and glasses in a main-building clinic. The medical staff consisted of a chief physician—second in command under the Harbor's governor—three interns, a ward master and assistant, nine nurses, and bedpan carriers. On a nursing-home level, medical facilities were first class, but patients who were acutely ill had to be transferred to more fully equipped and staffed institutions.

In the early days, church attendance was compulsory. Sunday was the one day of the week when the mariners could neither leave the grounds nor receive visitors. Men who did not choose to attend the in-house Presbyterian or Episcopalian services were permitted "to partake of the Lord's supper" in nearby New Brighton, but they had to return in time for the special Sunday roll call. Morning and evening prayers were said daily in the main hall of the center dormitory until 1856, when a plain Greek Revival chapel opened. A full-time chaplain had been recruited in 1848. In 1893, the chapel was superseded by the Randall Memorial Church, a lavish white marble building with a Florentine-style

dome and twin towers that became a Staten Island landmark. Theodore Dreiser was greatly impressed, especially with the interior's harmonious combination of marble and stained glass. The organ contained 2,300 pipes. According to Snug Harbor tradition, the church, with a seating capacity of 270, was one-sixth the size of London's St. Paul's Cathedral. Impressive as it was as a memorial to the founder of the Harbor, as a church it was fated to endure a history of lonely Sundays. Attendance was no longer compulsory, so fewer than 1 in 10 of the residents participated in Sunday services.[11]

Interior of the landmarked chapel.

Randall Memorial had a neighbor with no such attendance problems— the 600-seat music hall. Built at the same time and within a few dozen yards of each other, the two buildings—each with classical porticos of six Ionic columns—were creations of architect Robert Gibson. The music hall presented vaudeville acts; popular music programs; well-known speakers; and, beginning in 1911, twice-weekly showings of motion pictures. Among the long-forgotten entertainers were the Hotchkiss Sisters, the Hinddos Jugglers, Lovett's Boston Stars, and the Metropolitan Minstrels. In October 1899, one year after becoming the first to sail alone around the world, Joshua Slocum was the guest speaker.[12]

*Creating ship models for
sale to the public.*

Visitors often expressed surprise to find hundreds of old sailors
hard at work in the bright basement corridors weaving palm leaf and
rattan into rugs and mats, hammocks, and fishnets. Others produced
model ships sculpted by jackknife, and marine views painted on
seashells. For the less creative who wanted to work, Harbor management provided low-paying jobs for part-time guides, table waiters, and
farmhands. These activities helped the retired seamen combat what was
often a monotonous leisure and allowed them to earn small incomes that
provided for minor comforts not supplied by the Harbor. Each man
received a monthly tobacco ration, but no rum was dispensed even
though most of the men would have been satisfied with an occasional
nip. Some sent money home to children, and an old New Hampshire seaman acquired a private library of 40 volumes including a *History of
Julius Caesar* by Napoleon Bonaparte. Products from skilled hands were
sold to visitors and to at least two Manhattan stores that bought wholesale from the seamen. Business became so good that in 1923 the counsel
to the trustees warned that the manufacture and sale of goods on Harbor
grounds could result "in the withdrawal of the tax exemption." That legal
opinion slowed but did not completely stop the production of weaving,
carving, and painting for profit. By the 1950s, the retired seamen had

begun to receive Social Security and pension checks, and the tradition of producing arts and crafts for pin money faded away.

Sailors' Snug Harbor accepted its first guests five years before the ocean-steamship era opened in the port of New York with the dual arrival of the British liners *Great Western* and *Sirius* on April 23, 1838. It would be another dozen years before Yankee steamships would cross the ocean. Not surprisingly, the "old, decrepit and worn-out sailors" the trustees had in mind when they drew up standards of eligibility for residence in Randall's institution were seamen who raised and lowered sails, not the fellows who stoked furnaces or oiled engines.

In the 1880s, Robert Osborn and Edward Kelly, engine-room veterans no longer able to work because of injuries, were refused admission on the grounds that they were not sailors. Kelly had served nearly 40 years on steamers, and both he and Osborn had survived shipwrecks. Publicity surrounding their persistent but unsuccessful efforts to be accepted by the Harbor forced the trustees to expand their definition of the word sailor. They opened the gates for seamen who had served on steamships, deep-sea fishermen, and Great Lakes mariners who met the other requirements for entrance.

Seamen whose service was in sailing vessels—and into the 1940s

On wheels from kitchen to dining rooms. "Please no fruit or greens."

they still made up three-quarters of the residents—remained contemptuous of those who knew only steam. A legendary example of this animosity occurred on a winter morning in the early 1930s when Captain Martin Svendrup of the sailing-ship fraternity awakened to find his steamer roommate, Captain James Pigot, fiddling with the radiator. Suddenly the room was flooded with steam. "There'll be no steam in my room," shouted Svendrup, whacking Pigot over the head with his cane, and knocking him unconscious. Svendrup spent the next 11 days in the Richmond County jail. The judge who released him made an attempt to get the two old men to shake hands. Pigot agreed, but Svendrup stomped off indignantly.[13]

Svendrup and fellow veterans of square-rigged barks and brigs offer all kinds of reasons for looking with contempt on those whose sailing lives supposedly had been softer and safer because of steam. "Ghost fleet" maps, found in Cape Hatteras gift shops, show the sites of more than 500 wrecks, nearly all of them masted vessels, on or near the 180 nautical miles of the Outer Banks. That is enough to bring most landlubbers around to Svendrup's view.

The truth is that, while different, the modern mariner's life is neither safe nor easy. In *Looking for a Ship*, John McPhee's 1990 account of the American Merchant Marine, he quotes the captain of a container ship: "Every day, somewhere someone is getting it from the weather. They're running aground. They're hitting each other. They're disappearing without a trace." McPhee riffles through a dozen or so quarterly issues of *Mariners Weather Log*, published by the National Oceanic and Atmospheric Administration, chronicler of marine disasters throughout the world. By his quick count, 4 ships disappeared, 11 sank in rough seas, 9 capsized, 6 sank after collisions, 2 sank when their cargoes shifted, an iceberg sank 1 ship and lightening sank another, and 5 ships ran aground in fog. More than 300 crew members were lost in these disasters.[14] A report from Lloyd's Registry of Shipping in the *New York Times* of March 16, 1999, tells a frightening maritime story. From 1980 to 1998, the sea claimed 180 gigantic bulk carriers—nearly 1 a month—and 1,465 lives. If most readers were surprised, perhaps it was because these haulers of ore, grain, and coal to ports around the world nearly always sail under such flags as Cyprus, Liberia, and Panama with crews from poor nations.

The Old Stone Jug Tavern, a saloon where Theodore Dreiser may have chatted with the old sailors, was two blocks east of the main gate

Earning pin money by weaving palm leaf into baskets.

on Richmond Terrace. A retired sea captain, John Neville, built it in 1770 as his residence. With its long verandah overlooking the Kill, the Jug was an inviting place to take a pint. It was also the occasional site of a rumpus. Trustee minutes of June 2, 1898, record such an incident. Resident Frank Ross and a couple of buddies were discussing the good work of the ladies employed by the Harbor when an outsider interrupted to say that there was not a virtuous woman inside the gates. Ross, claiming complete sobriety, challenged the remarks and got badly beaten up as a consequence. Dazed, he staggered back to the Harbor for medical aid. The gatekeeper said he was drunk. Ross told the governor he was willing to be restricted but asked that his name be left off the curfew list "so that I will not be held up to ridicule." He was let off with a warning.[15]

Yo Ho Ho and a Bottle . . .

Was it rum, maritime novelist Patrick O'Brien asked, or the unnatural cloistered life that made sailors regard the land as Fiddler's Green, that perpetual holiday where the fiddler never stops for dancers who never tire? In either case was rum the demon that so many stories about Sailors' Snug Harbor make it out to be? Captain John Whetten, the institution's first governor, called a special meeting of the trustees on June 1, 1836, to complain: "The injunction forbidding ardent spirits is set at naught inasmuch as there is scarcely a day allowed to pass without indications of intemperance, insubordination, and wrangling. . . . There have

For retired travelers,
a reading room with
a timely collection
of international
newspapers.

been recent incidence of individuals having being found beastly drunk upon the road and brought home by strangers to the disgrace of the institution and the mortification of the sober part of its members." Whetten suspected that "the rum drinkers who came here without money or credit ... obtained the means for their poison" by selling articles stolen from the farm. The trustees agreed that such offenders would be "summarily expelled." A few meetings later, Whetten, a religious man and a strict disciplinarian, reported that "the house has been orderly and quiet" since violators of the drinking rules had found punishment swift and certain.

The governor still was not content with the ways of his wards, however. In 1842, he ordered construction of a seven-foot fence around 20 acres of the northern boundary of the Harbor. This proved a challenge to many of the old-timers, who quickly demonstrated that they could still scale seven feet in a jiffy. Although it may not have been much of an obstruction, the fence, in good shape to this day, was a handsome cast-iron ornament whose design was inspired by the Cumberland Gates of London's Hyde Park.

Whetten's successor in 1845 was Captain Fred Augustus Depeyster, who expected to check the temptation to imbibe spirits by providing a ration of cider. The experiment ended quickly when some of the men were accused of trading their cider outside the gate for rum.

Neither Whetten nor Depeyster had much in common with former tenants of the fo'castle. Both were wealthy China hands. For many years, Depeyster commanded John Jacob Astor's celebrated *Beaver*, which once cleared a $200,000 profit on a single voyage. As president of The Marine Society and father-in-law of a Brevoort, Whetten was a member of the city's best business and social circles. At sea, both Harbor governors were undoubtedly accustomed to instant obedience. Flogging ensured strict discipline in those days, although we have no way of knowing if either skipper ever ordered a scourging. Even Dana, whose book is in good part an indictment of the cruelties of merchant captains, wrote that he would not command a ship without holding up the threat of flogging. Finally in 1850, flogging was abolished by an act of Congress.

Crimping, another tradition that did nothing to prepare common seamen for polite society, lasted considerably longer. Old Cap Knowles, as he is called by author Frank Waters in *Eight Bells: Sailors' Snug Harbor Yarns and Ballads,* tells how as a young man he was drugged and shanghaied in a Water Street saloon by a stranger who promised him

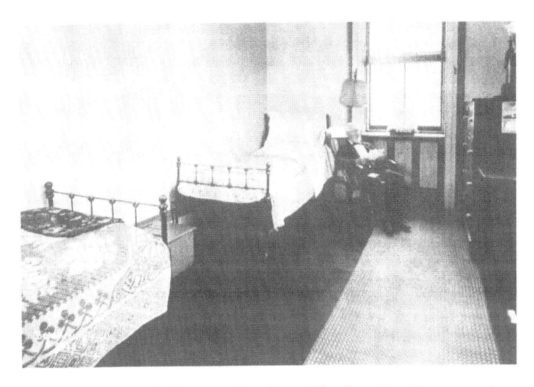

Comfortable quarters for two, even when sharing a single dresser.

a berth on a coasting schooner. When he awakened, he was on a three-masted ship headed for Rangoon and compelled "to work off three months of hard earned wages advanced to a damn crimp I didn't owe a cent to." Because shipmasters for whom the crimps worked monopolized the recruiting of deep-water hands, shipowners found it difficult or impossible to secure crews unless they paid the recruiters a shamelessly large percentage of prospective wages. A congressional act in June 1884 struck at the roots of the system by prohibiting advance wages and providing that wage allotments be made only to near relatives.[16]

The Social Security Act of 1935 established a federal system of old-age retirement insurance and a federal-state system of unemployment insurance for most American wage earners, but not for merchant seamen. Benefits were not extended to them until four years later.

Congressional indifference to the welfare of seamen was even more marked in the GI Bill of Rights, which guaranteed home loans and paid college tuition for millions of World War II veterans. Congress refused to accept the crews of merchant ships as deserving veterans, despite testimony from the War Shipping Administration that "the percentage of casualties in the merchant marine . . . [was] three or four times that of

*Snack time at
"The Bumboat."*

the armed forces." In response to the argument that seamen were highly paid to take risks, the administration presented comparisons showing
that deckhands and noncommissioned officers received similar pay,
whether they served on navy or merchant vessels. The testimony concluded with this statement: "Every man serving aboard a merchant vessel, with the possible exception of the master and the chief engineer,
could earn more money in a shipyard or defense plant without taking
the chance of being killed."[17] Belated recognition of merchant sailors as
veterans came in May 1988 when they were made eligible to participate
in the Veterans Administration's health-care system.

Unlicensed seamen's efforts to form labor unions dated to the 1850s
in New York, but the impact of organized labor on wages and conditions
was mostly subliminal until the massive maritime strikes of the 1930s
resulted in the formation of the Seafarers' International and the National
Maritime Union. The unions negotiated health and welfare plans in 1949
and 1950, and shortly after this they negotiated pension plans.[18]

At Sailors' Snug Harbor itself, the negative term *inmates*, always
used when referring to the men, was abandoned in the 1930s in favor
of *mariners*. Earlier, an effort was made to address all residents by the

honorary title of captain. Many residents objected, at least in part, because they were content with being an engineer or a boatswain.

Because of the demise of flogging and crimping and the advent of insurance and pensions, the sea began to treat its followers more kindly. And because of that, reports of drunkenness among sailors began to diminish. Captain Thomas Melville, as obsessed as his predecessors with the drinking problem when he became the Harbor's third governor in 1867, reported with great pleasure in 1878 that although the institution's population had increased by a quarter to 600, "there was less dissatisfaction, drunkenness and disorderly conduct during the past year, than in any one year since I have been in charge." One of Melville's successors reported "not one case of intoxication" during the New Year's holiday of 1902. Some years later, another governor told a reporter for the *New Yorker*, "If we had 875 ministers or lawyers here, we'd have just as much drinking."

By 1970, cocktail parties on Harbor grounds were held for the mariners on such special occasions as the Fourth of July and Christmas.

Today, wine and beer is served at weekly happy hours and during monthly parties and banquets. Many of the men keep drinks of their choice in their rooms.

The Governors

Captain John Whetten, governor of Sailors' Snug Harbor from 1833 to 1844, was a young first mate on the *Experiment* in 1785 when it became the second American ship that sailed to China. At 85 tons, the little sloop was less than a quarter the size of its bellwether in the China trade, the *Empress of China*. Whetten would later command some of the finest ships sailing from New York. In 1825, he was appointed president of The Marine Society and a trustee of the Harbor, positions he held for 20 years. During that time, The Marine Society, founded in 1770 to care for distressed shipmasters or their widows and children and to promote nautical knowledge, was among New York's premier organizations. Every merchant captain of substance was a

John Whetten, first of the retired sea captains to serve as Harbor governor (1833-44).

member, and nearly all men of importance on Wall Street and South Street were active honorary members. The election of a Marine Society captain to the position of governor of Sailors' Snug Harbor became a tradition that lasted 136 years, but for one 10-year period when the governor came from the officer ranks of the U.S. Navy. The first three in the row of five Greek Revival buildings were built on Whetten's watch. He resigned in September 1844, probably because of age. Harbor physician Stephen Begert served as acting superintendent until June 1845, when Captain Depeyster came aboard. Begert continued as the Harbor's chief physician until 1882.[19]

Captain Fred Augustus Depeyster, governor from 1845 to 1867, may have been more popular with the men than Whetten, judged by the number of anecdotes that circulated about his career. For example, Depeyster's ship was one of many anchored in the Whampoa Reach, the port of Canton, when a sailor fell headlong from a British vessel into the rushing tideway. Depeyster dived from his quarterdeck and grasped the struggling tar by the hair. Before a small boat reached them, a powerful current carried the two men toward the sea, but the captain held onto his man. Depeyster was a hero to his fellow skippers—many came aboard to shake his hand—and to hundreds of seamen and coolies who cheered the rescue. Then there was the time that the *Columbus* was caught in the severest of gales off the coast of Wales. Thundering waves threatened to drive the ship onto the rocky coast. But, the story goes, "by a most admirable display of seamanship, Captain Depeyster saved his vessel." He was the first to live in the 30-room governor's mansion, which was well to the west on the great lawn and a bit closer to the shore than the dormitory row.

More is known about Captain Thomas Melville, Harbor governor from 1867 to 1884, than any governor before modern times. This is because he kept a log of his quarterly reports to the trustees for those 17 years, which is in the archives. In addition, he was the youngest and favorite brother of author Herman Melville and therefore subject to a fair amount of publicity.

Thomas Melville, Harbor governor (1867–84). He was the best known of the early governors, in part because of his brother Herman.

In 1846 at age 16, Thomas Melville went whaling. Eventually, he skippered a number of ships in the Pacific including the clipper *Bengal Tiger*. When he returned to New York from a voyage in 1860, he found a dejected big brother; the novels Herman wrote after *Moby Dick* in 1851 had been failures. Tom invited him to be his companion on a voyage around Cape Horn to San Francisco and Shanghai aboard the *Meteor*. Herman, who had spent a couple of his early years at sea soaking up lore for his novels, accepted. Several weeks into the voyage, the *Meteor* was run down by a mishandled British brig and nearly sunk. After it limped into San Francisco, Herman headed back to New York, where he would support his family as a customs clerk while continuing a writing career that produced his tragic masterpiece, *Billy Budd*, a few months before his death in 1891.

Thomas Melville was 37 in 1867 when he was elected to serve as the third governor of the Harbor, despite protests from The Marine Society. Although he was a native New Yorker and a veteran shipmaster, he had never bothered to join The Marine Society, and his peers did not like the snub. Melville obviously tried to amend this oversight. He appears on the membership list as number 2905, October 12, 1868.

Melville came to the Harbor as a bachelor. Shortly after his arrival, he began courting Catherine Begart, daughter of the institution's long-serving chief physician. They married on June 6, 1868. In her biography of Herman Melville, Laurie Robertson-Lorant writes: "The year 1868 drew to a festive close when nine Melvilles and eight Begarts converged for Christmas dinner at Sailors' Snug Harbor. . . . Thomas' life at Snug Harbor was comfortable and pleasant. He liked to show off with lavish hospitality as did Catherine her exemplary Dutch housekeeping."[20]

Taboo, a South Pacific word that became part of Harbor lingo, was introduced by Melville and frequently applied by him. Someone tabooed for breaking a rule might be restricted to the grounds for a few days or weeks or lose his tobacco ration. More than a taboo would be needed to correct the problem that Melville reported to the trustees on September 28, 1868. A group of inmates had pooled their money, hired a lawyer, and were preparing to sue the officers for swindling Harbor funds and the trustees for squandering money. These charges were based on the belief that Sailors' Snug Harbor belonged individually to the inmates, and that the officers and trustees were their servants and had no right to enforce bylaws or to expel residents. The mariners lost their case in court, and the principal proponents of the defeated theory were expelled. One of them, Charles Newman, attempted to shoot board president Captain John Ferrier. Captain Ferrier wrestled the loaded pistol away from Newman, who was sentenced to five years in prison for felonious assault. Not long after he had completed his sentence, the homeless former convict applied for readmission to the Harbor. He was turned down but, at the trustees' expense, a place was found for him in the Seaman's Retreat.

Melville had another, less vexing problem with the men. He wanted them to do chores such as helping the steward to hang the wash, sweeping the walks, and helping out on the farm—all without pay. They would not do it and they finally won out. The trustees agreed to pay at a rate of 20 cents a day—not bad when compared to a matron's pay of 55 cents a day.

Melville's biggest problem was one he brought on himself. The Harbor treasurer accused him in 1872 of embezzling funds and of general mismanagement or carelessness in the purchase of supplies. The trustees formed an investigating committee that took 200 pages of testimony from employees and vendors. It turned out that Melville kept sloppy expense accounts and that he had taken chickens, milk, and bread for his family without paying. He offered full payment for any errors or omissions in his accounts, but he argued that he deserved the produce for services performed beyond his official duties. Although the trustees did not agree with his premise, they concluded that he was not guilty of embezzlement. What did concern them was Melville's purchasing practices. The time had come, they decided, to relieve him of some of his duties by creating an administrative office on Greene Street in Manhattan to handle all Harbor purchases and finances and its Manhattan leases and rentals.

During Melville's tenure, the Harbor population more than doubled to more than 800, and the front-five Greek Revival row was completed. The trustees' confidence in Melville's management of the fast-expanding institution was expressed at each election. But he never seemed to win the respect of the old mariners. One of them, who had enough of Harbor life after 18 months, published an unsigned pamphlet in 1879. His complaints covered the food, taboos, the residents' idleness, and the manner in which the Harbor was run. About the governor, he wrote, "The prevailing opinion is that his position could be better served by someone else." Melville died unexpectedly of a heart attack in March 1884.

Gustavus D. S. Trask, Harbor governor (1884-98). The nickname "Bulldog" may explain why he was dismissed as governor.

Gustavus D. S. Trask, fourth governor of Sailors' Snug Harbor, was born into one of the earliest families of Salem, Massachusetts, in 1837. He was a graduate of Hamilton Collegiate Institute and had served as master of several first-class merchant ships operating between New York and Liverpool. In 1877 the captain wrote, in rolling Victorian style, the first brief history of The Marine Society of the City of New York. For several years before succeeding Melville at the Harbor, he was marine surveyor for the New York Board of Underwriters.

Captain Trask took office just in time to organize unveiling ceremonies for the nine-foot, bronze statue of Robert Richard Randall, sculpted by Augustus Saint Gaudens for a fee of $10,000. That may have been the pleasantest time of his 14-year career at the Harbor. He quickly earned the nickname "Bulldog" and a reputation as an even stricter disciplinarian than his predecessors.

A voting scandal burst over the Harbor in the spring of 1889. The trustees had decided to look into rumors about vote buying in a Richmond County election, very much a possibility at a time when Richard Croker, Grand Sachem of Tammany Hall, and Republican Party "Boss" Tom Platt were in a fierce struggle for control of political offices on all New York electoral levels. More than 500 old seamen were questioned at secret hearings. It is reported that half of them admitted frankly that they had been paid for their votes in recent elections. Even though the testimony suggested that the Harbor had become a market for the buying and selling of votes, a general amnesty was declared for those who had simply received bribes. But Trask was ordered to expel some ring leaders and suspend others.

Requests from several newspapers and the Associated Press for permission to attend the hearings were refused. The *New York Times* took the matter into its own hands by interviewing a score of the punished seamen. The result was a series of articles in June 1889 charging that Trask was attempting to "control the franchise" of the 800 Harbor residents. According to the *Times*, "Governor Trask is a Republican who believes that a man of any other political belief is devoid of all sense of Honor.... Invariably, the majority of the inmates voted Democratic until the 1888 presidential election when they favored the Republican, Benjamin Harrison." The switch in parties was attributed to "fear of Trask [who] during his four years of governorship has exercised a tyranny." The local election that inspired the spring investigation went to the Democrats by some 400 votes. That result, the *Times* reported, led "Trask to charge that the votes had been bought.... All the dismissed are Democrats with unblemished records at Sailors' Snug Harbor." The trustees ignored the newspaper assaults on Trask and expressed their confidence in him "as an efficient and honest executive."

On a Sunday evening the following December 8, as Trask walked alone from the Harbor train station to his residence, one of the men who had been dismissed in the spring, Enoch Anderson, fired three shots from a 38-caliber revolver at the governor, hitting him once. The bullet lodged in a bundle of papers in the left-hand breast pocket of Trask's overcoat, causing only a slight abrasion. Anderson told the police that he had become a homeless wanderer on the streets of New York because of Trask.[21]

Problems of a different stripe arose in 1892 when Staten Island representatives pushed a bill through both houses of the state legislature that would deprive charitable institutions of school tax exemptions if they earned an annual income in excess of $200,000 in real and personal income. In a special hearing before New York Governor Roswell P. Flowers, the trustees pointed out that the Harbor was the specific target of the bill because it would affect no other institution. Despite the trustees' argument, Flowers signed the bill the next day.

The assessed valuation of Harbor property on Staten Island in June 1892, according to the village of New Brighton, was $384,000. The actual tax paid was $25,259.52. The assessment doubled to $768,000 in 1893. The New Brighton supervisor told an inquiring trustee that public clamor had been so great that he and the assessors had no choice but to approve the increase. The trustees refused to pay, and the matter was disputed in the courts until 1901 when the annual assessment stood at $1,228,600. On June 25, the state supreme court vacated and canceled all assessments on the Staten Island property for 1899. William Allaire Shortt, who had argued the case for the Harbor, informed the trustees that with the exemption established he would be able to procure additional judgments against the assessments and taxes for other years.

The Reverend Morgan Dix, rector of Trinity Church and trustee of Sailors' Snug Harbor for more than four decades beginning in the Civil War.

As Harbor Governor, Trask had no role in the battle over assessments, taxes, and exemptions, but he almost surely felt pressure from the administrative uncertainties it caused. Another unrelated, unexpected, and unexplained matter was to have a devastating impact on his career. This strange situation arose in October 1897. An assistant physician, Dr. Brandon Richardson, charged his chief, Dr. H. D. Jay, with incompetence and challenged the board of trustees to investigate the way in which the hospital was being run. A committee of inquiry met on November 4 and requested both doctors and Governor Trask to testify. In addition, two mariners, two nurses, and the Harbor engineer were called by the panel. No explanation appears in the minutes about what was expected from them. Captain Crawford, one of the mariners, began by telling how he had been mistreated by the governor. Immediately, a panel member offered a motion noting that the only object of the hearing was to investigate charges against the chief physician. The motion was overruled, and Crawford continued to tell his story. At the next meeting, on November 9, a former inmate, Timothy Whelan, requested and was granted permission to testify about Harbor matters. Before Whelan could be examined, Trask declared that he wanted to be represented by counsel. He hired Vernon M. Davis to represent him, and the trustees appointed Frank Moss as their special counsel. Nowhere is there even a hint of why the lawyers were needed.

From November 4, 1897, through the following January 7, the investigating panel held 25 meetings and questioned 132 witnesses, some of them more than once. On December 29, each lawyer delivered 1-hour summations before the board itself. Immediately thereafter, the

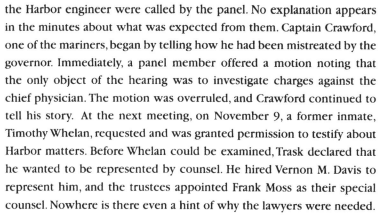

board met in executive session to read a letter from the Reverend
Morgan Dix, the long-time Trinity Church trustee who had been ill. Dix
wrote:

> It would be unbecoming to ask of my colleagues that they
> should not take final action in the enforced absence of the old-
> est member of the Board: but if action could be postponed, it
> would be most gratifying to me. . . .
> I deem it certain that a change in the office of Governor will
> shortly be made. I am certain that this is the wish of at least
> three of my colleagues. . . . Such a change must be made, either
> at the time of the next annual election, or prior to that time, by
> way of a decree of removal from office. I earnestly hope that
> the change will not be made until the termination of the cur-
> rent official year; and I shall not by voice or vote oppose it then
> if that course be adopted. But I implore the Board by every
> consideration that should influence kind-hearted and thought-
> ful men, not to take the latter course. The present Governor has
> served the Institution thirteen years, as I believe, with great
> ability and intention to do his duty faithfully, as he understood
> it, not without fault or errors, but upon the whole, in a manner
> that entitles him to the credit of being the ablest Governor
> since the foundation of the Institution. To terminate his course
> abruptly by infliction of the most severe punishment which
> the Board has the power to award and to send him forth, short-
> ly before the regular termination of his appointed term, with a
> stigma on his name and sorrow in his heart and in those of his
> family and friends, would be an act unworthy of ourselves, and
> not justified by the evidence.

Despite Dix's eloquent plea, a resolution offered by the Reverend
Howard Duffield of First Presbyterian Church was approved with two
abstentions, the captains from The Marine Society. It read: "It is the judgment of the Board of Trustees that the Administration of the Sailors'
Snug Harbor should be changed as soon as it can be." Why the need for
this drastic change just three months before the governor's term was to
expire? No explanation appeared in the resolution, or elsewhere. At the
next meeting, January 7, 1898, the board accepted Captain Trask's resignation, dated January 4.

On January 14, the board received a petition signed by 23 prominent physicians that urged the retention of Dr. Jay. The charges against him were dismissed by a four-to-two vote. Meanwhile, Richardson, the instigator, had left the Harbor some months earlier.

The Trask saga did not quite end with his resignation. The executive committee refused his June 1898 request for reimbursement of the $2,000 he had spent on legal and stenographic services. But in July, when his two principal foes, Duffield and City Recorder John W. Goff, were on vacation, the summer executive committee recommended payment and the trustees approved it. This could have eased what might have been an embarrassing face-off 18 months later when Trask, who had become a Harbor trustee as the newly elected president of The Marine Society, attended a board meeting. After a single year in office, Trask stepped aside to update and enlarge The Marine Society history that he had written 25 years earlier. He died in 1914 at age 77.

A search committee would not be needed to find a new governor, because the team of Goff and Duffield had a candidate in mind even before Trask resigned. He was Lieutenant Commander Daniel Delehanty of the U.S. Navy, at the time executive officer of the battleship *Texas* and a veteran of nearly 40 years at sea. Delehanty was elected at the board meeting on January 14, 1898, but not without a struggle. In separate nominations, Captain George Norton proposed and Captain Austin Jayne seconded the names of 10 Marine Society captains. All lost before Goff brought Delehanty's name into consideration, with a second from Duffield.

The Marine Society made its disapproval of the election official in a series of resolutions that were sent to U.S. Navy Secretary John D. Long. He was informed that tradition and the character of the Harbor called for the office of governor to be filled by a shipmaster from the merchant marine, rather than someone in the paid service of the government. Delehanty received a salary of $5,000 as governor and $2,300 as a naval officer. The society charged that Delehanty's election was "brought about by the influence with some Trustees of Senator Murphy of Troy, father-in-law of the present governor, who got Assistant Secretary Theodore Roosevelt to authorize the detail."

Secretary Long asked the trustees for comment. In their six-page reply, the trustees noted that "trustees are absolutely independent of the bodies to which they belong," that members of The Marine Society had been elected in the past by the Trustees "in the free exercise of their appointive powers," and that neither Randall's will nor the Harbor charter "give the Society the privilege of supplying the governor of Sailors' Snug Harbor." They went on to say, "Your correspondents are amazed at the suggestion that political motives were involved. . . . The charge is without foundation."

The Marine Society's view about filling Harbor posts had been spelled out a few weeks earlier when a search committee was instructed to hire a new chief for the steward's department "purely on merits without regard to personal preferences or sympathies." In a minority report, Captain Norton wrote, "preferences in appointments should be given to Mariners for all places they are competent to fill. I believe this was the intent of Captain Randall and has been the custom until quite recently."

Delehanty's installation as governor took place in January in the newly opened music hall before an assembly of old mariners. He was still learning the ropes when called back to active navy duty at the outbreak of the Spanish-American War. Captain George W. Brown, The Marine Society's first choice to succeed Trask, was named acting governor. Delehanty was skipper of the *Sewanee* when it ran the blockade before the forts of Santiago Harbor. He returned to the Harbor in October as a full commander and a hero.

Delehanty's report to the trustees about the state of the Harbor when he assumed the duties of governor turns out to be a severe condemnation of Trask, although the dismissed man's name is not mentioned. "I found the Harbor in a disorganized and demoralized state," Delehanty wrote. "The inmates divided into warring factions; unnecessary rules in force and restrictions that keep the inmates in a constant state of discontent; and the rules and regulations to promote their comfort disregarded."

In Delehanty's first months in office, administrative actions and reforms began to win warm respect from the men as well as the trustees. The new governor abolished what he considered unnecessary rules and restrictions, installed a system of accounts in the steward's department that resulted in better food and less waste, and increased efficiency by adding 2 electrical engineers and 18 other employees to the staff. The number of mariners on the Harbor payroll rose from 102 to 199 after Delehanty found that a good bit of inmate discontent was caused by idleness.

The medical center caught Delehanty's sharpest attention. He reported to the trustees that many men, even when seriously ill, refused to go to the hospital because of alleged neglect and ill treatment at the hands of the male nurses. After careful observation, he had come to agree with the men's complaints. When the governor discussed the situation with Dr. Jay, he was "met with opposition and indifference." As a result, Jay, citing illness, soon retired, and Delehanty took the helm of the hospital in his own hands. He inspected at odd hours and impressed upon the staff that neglect or indifference would not be tolerated. A major part of his reorganization plan was the addition of 11 nurses so that the longest shift could be cut from 16 to 8 hours.

Delehanty was not surprised to read in the *New York Herald* one morning that 10 nurses, including 2 that he had fired, were preparing a complaint for the trustees charging that the governor interfered improperly with hospital management, and that he disturbed the nurses and their patients by entering the wards at all hours, noisily, and at times drunkenly. Delehanty immediately requested a board investigation. He stated, "Efforts to bring about the necessary reforms have aroused vindictive opposition in those whose interests lie in the failure of my administration." Captain Norton was the target of that remark, for as the investigation would show, he clearly had a hand in publicizing the complaints of the nurses. At the end of a two-month probe, the investigating committee, which included the other Marine Society captain, Austin Jayne, found unanimously that the charges "are not only without foundation, but should be branded maliciously false."

Not long after his name was cleared, Delehanty formally retired from the navy. He governed a serene Harbor until November 1907, when seriously impaired health forced him to step down. He was named governor emeritus with an annual pension of $3,000.

Captain Andrew Newbury, president of The Marine Society and a trustee for seven years, moved into the governor's mansion in January 1908. Joining the board around the same time were three new members, Chamber of Commerce President J. Edward Simmons; Newbury's replacement, Captain A. W. Smith; and Dr. William T. Manning, who had become rector of Trinity Church upon the death of Morgan Dix, a trustee for 42 years.

A dozen residents quickly tested the mettle of the new order by calling on the governor and the board to render an account of Harbor business dealings since 1898. In addition, they demanded to see a "true" copy of the Randall will and they filed a series of complaints with the state board of charity. A bulletin posted on January 10, 1910, contained the trustee's answer. An investigation, it said, uncovered organized insubordination that attempted to spread discontent and to create contempt for authority. Because some conspirers were more guilty than others, punishments differed in severity. Three residents were expelled and nine were tabooed for periods ranging from one year to three months. The other memorable event during Newbury's 11 years of governance was the presentation of stained-glass windows to the Randall Memorial Church in June 1915.

Captain George E. Beckwith, decorated for bravery under fire at Santiago in the Spanish-American War and a World War I naval officer, took over the governor's office in May 1919. During his tenure, the board rewrote the strict bylaws into a more liberal set of rules. In the new Harbor, old sailors were to enjoy the fullest liberty and self-respect "consistent with good order and a due regard for the peace and comfort of the community." It was Beckwith who equated for the *New Yorker* the drinking habits of his crew of retired mariners with those of ministers and lawyers. His encouragement inspired three residents to publish books: Frank Waters,

GOVERNORS OF THE SAILORS' SNUG HARBOR	
1. John Whetten	August 1833 — September 1844
2. Fred Augustus Depeyster	June 1845 — November 1867
3. Thomas Melville	November 1867 — March 1884
4. Gustavus D.S. Trask	March 1884 — January 1898
5. Daniel Delehanty	January 1898 — January 1908
6. Andrew J. Newbury	January 1908 — May 1919
7. George E. Beckwith	May 1919 — November 1934
8. Howard A. Flynn	January 1935 — June 1947
9. Henry R. Patterson	November 1947 — September 1952
10. Charles C. Baldwin	October 1952 — January 1955
11. William Twig	November 1955 — October 1961
12. Sidney Trew	April 1962 — June 1969
13. Leo Kraszeski	June 1969 — June 1987
14. James Watters	July 1987 — June 1988
15. Thomas Katsanis	August 1988 — May 1990
16. Patrick Ausband	November 1990 — Present

who went to sea as a teenager in the 1860s, wrote *Eight Bells: Sailors' Snug Harbor Yarns and Ballads*; William Morris Barnes recounted his adventures in *When Ships Were Ships and Not Tin Pots*; and O.W. Hicks wrote *Sea Tales from Sailors' Snug Harbor*. All three publications were dedicated to Beckwith, who was stricken with a heart attack in November 1934 and died.

Captain Howard A. Flynn succeeded Beckwith in January 1935. He was a captain at 21, master of several schooners before becoming commander of a navy steamer in World War I, a vice president of The Marine Society, and port captain of the C. D. Mallory Steamship Company before resigning to become governor at one of the most difficult periods in

Snug Harbor's history. Because of the depression, the Harbor's legendary wealth fell to the point where expenses exceeded income. Every bed was filled, and an unknown number of eligible applicants were turned away. In April 1940, the trustee minutes noted: "Since the coming of Flynn there has been an increasing sensitivity to the needs of the community." Flynn's thoughtfulness inspired tranquillity in a time of turbulence and an understanding among his charges about how fortunate they were to be inside the Harbor's gates.

Flynn retired in 1947 at the age of 61 and was replaced by Captain Henry R. Patterson, age 65. The new governor first went to sea on a sailing ship and served on a navy steamship in World War I before joining Jarka Corporation, one of the largest stevedoring firms, where he remained for 25 years. Patterson was elected president of The Marine Society in January 1942, one month before he was recalled by the navy for active duty.

When Patterson retired in September 1952, Captain Charles C. Baldwin, president of The Marine Society, replaced him. Baldwin had been the top marine superintendent of United Fruit in the United States and manager of its terminal operations in the North Atlantic. He died in January 1955.

Frank L. Hickock, assistant manager of the Harbor's real estate department who had never been to sea, filled in as temporary governor until the appointment of Captain William C. Twig in November. Twig, who skippered a troop transport in World War II, had been assistant to the operating vice president of the Grace Line. At 50, he was younger than most past governors and, although a member of The Marine Society, he had never served as president. In 1958 the new office of director and chief executive officer was created and filled by a hospital administrator. The governor reported to him. The minutes do not make clear what happened next. Twig may have taken a long sick leave. He died in March 1962.

Captain Sidney Trew became governor in April 1962. He was an Englishman who went to sea at 16 and received his British master's license at 23. Ten years later he qualified for an American license. He had been an executive with the New York shipping board before coming to the Harbor. He resigned in June 1969.

Captain Leo Kraszeski succeeded Trew. He was the last member of The Marine Society to serve as governor. His 18 stimulating years in office and those of his successors are covered in chapter 9.

Notes

1. The *Staten Island Advance* published a five-part reprint of Dreiser's report about Sailors' Snug Harbor during the week beginning Monday, August 15, 1977.

2. James C. Healey, *Foc's'le and Glory Hole*, p. 12.

3. Flynn and the *New York Herald-Tribune*, January 27, 1935.

4. Herman Melville, *Moby Dick*, p. 1.

5. Richard Henry Dana Jr., *Two Years before the Mast*, p. 462.

6. Samuel Samuels, *From the Forecastle to the Cabin*, see chapter 13 for the harem rescue, chapter 16 for the pirates, and chapter 19 for the *Dreadnought*, "built especially for me."

7. Dana, *Two Years before the Mast*, p. 470.

8. Samuel Eliot Morison's views about Yankee seamen begin on page 106 of his *Maritime History of Massachusetts, 1783-1860*.

9. Jeffrey W. Bolster, *Black Jacks*, pp. 235-9.

10. Many of the anecdotes on these pages were culled from magazine feature stories in *Harper's*, December 1872; *Century*, May 1884; and the New Yorker, October 1933. Captain Roberts's *Wavertree* memories appeared in *Sea History*, winter 1980-81.

11. Along with material from the Fort Schuyler files, a visit to the harbor includes reports from *Sea Tales*, written by Harbor resident O. W. Hicks in 1935; a 1908 feature in the *Independent;* a 1966 article in the *Staten Island Historian* called "Melville's Staten Island Paradise"; and clippings from the *Staten Island Advance*.

12. The music hall programs were recalled by the *Staten Island Advance* on May 29, 1978.

13. A discussion of sail versus steam appeared in *The Saturday Evening Post*, June 15, 1940.

14. John McPhee's account of what he found in the *Mariners Weather Log* appears in *Looking for a Ship*, p. 139.

15. The Old Stone Jug is described on page 617 of Federal Writers Project, *The WPA Guide to New York*. The Frank Ross incident appears in the June 2, 1898, minutes of a trustee meeting.

16. The demise of flogging and crimping is reported by Elmo Paul Hohman in *A History of American Merchant Seamen*, pp. 21-2.

17. Testimony by the War Shipping Administration is reported in Charles Dana Gibson, *Merchantmen? Or Ships of War*, pp. 147-8.

18. For unions, welfare, and pension plans, see Joseph P. Goldberg, *The Maritime Story: A Study in Labor-Management Relations*.

19. The archives provided most of the background for the pages about the governors. Beginning in the 1930s, clippings from the *Staten Island Advance* reported on Snug Harbor activities.

20. Information about Governor Thomas Melville appears in Laurie Robertson-Lorant's *Melville*, a biography about Thomas's elder brother Herman (pp. 88, 415–22, 476, and 573).

21. The attempt on Trask's life was reported on the front page of the *New York Tribune*, December 9, 1889.

PULLING DOWN AND BUILDING UP

"The whole of New York is rebuilt about once in ten years," wrote Philip Hone in 1836.[1] That observation by the eminent diarist was accurate enough to explain the staggering problem faced by Sailors' Snug Harbor in the second half of the nineteenth century because of its 21-year residential leases.

Bond and Bleecker Streets, just off Broadway, had become the city's most fashionable residential neighborhood by the mid 1830s. Less than a generation later the world of commerce had taken over the area, causing its wealthy inhabitants to decamp for Fifth Avenue, Gramercy Park, or other havens to the north. Boarding houses filled with immigrants, barrooms, and sweatshops, and a row of dentists and midwives took over the partitioned rows of Federal-style houses. Broadway's transformation from residential avenue to the clamorous center of elegant trade and entertainment was confirmed with the opening in 1862 of A.T. Stewart's shopping palace between Ninth and Tenth Streets, Broadway, and Fourth Avenue.

Beginning in 1854, Stewart bought up some 20 expiring leases that had yielded an aggregate rent of $5,220, then surrendered them to Harbor trustees. They in turn leased the entire square block to Stewart

A. T. Stewart. With money, patience, and foresight, he brought together a square block of leasehold lots on which to build his department store.

for 21 years, with the privilege of renewal, at an annual rent of $12,000 for the first four years and $36,000 for each of the remaining 17 years.

Stewart, unfortunately for the trustees, was one of a kind. No one else seemed to have the money, the patience, or the foresight to see that continuing to lease small lots for long terms was a mistake that would blight much of the old Minto farm area. When the wholesale garment trade crossed Canal on Broadway and neighboring streets after the Civil War, factory lofts of six or more stories replaced the old houses. The growth of this flourishing manufacturing district stopped at the southern edge of Harbor property. Businessmen who expected the stretch of Broadway from Canal to Union Square to develop into the mercantile center of the city attacked the trustees bitterly. "How do you account for the wretched condition of many parts of Broadway?" Henry Morton Robinson asked in a *Reader's Digest* article many years after the complaints began. The answer, he said, could be summed up in a single word, "obsolescence." Sailors' Snug Harbor, "the largest realty taxpayer in New York City," and its leases were blamed for much of the decay. "No bank will loan money on a short-term lease," Robinson wrote. "Purchasers can get no other title— so nothing ever happens. The buildings deteriorate, equipment becomes obsolescent, and the progressive tenants move out."

Despite the complaints, there was little the board could do immediately about the situation. The second tier of 21-year leases began to come due in 1872, but it would be another decade before the last of them expired. Assembling individual lots into large building plots was impracticable because of the timing of the expiration dates. East Tenth Street was typical. Leases for numbers 38 and 44 expired in 1872, the adjoining 40 and 42 in 1879. The exorbitant prices demanded by leaseholders for the sale of their unexpired contracts frightened off would-be buyers such as Roger Peet & Co., prestigious maker of men's clothing, which sought space for a factory. Like others, Peet skipped over the Harbor property to build farther uptown.

By repossessing "desirable" lots and spending "surplus" funds, the trustees were able to erect eight commercial buildings between 1879 and 1902 on Broadway, Astor Place, University Place, Greene Street, and Mercer Street. Only three remain, but they demonstrate that the trustees went first class with their property improvements. The building at 746–50 Broadway, built in 1881, is seven stories of robust Victorian red brick, one-half facing Broadway and the other Astor Place. The address is now 1 Astor Place. The buildings at 258-60 Greene Street, immediately south of the Harbor's Manhattan headquarters, and 297-303 Mercer Street are stately six-story sisters, each with two stories of rusticated limestone topped by four floors of gray brick. Today, they stand as a single apartment house with the main entrance on Mercer.

The trustees' building campaign—designed, with little success, to inspire similar property improvements by their lessees—had been too little and too late. Industry had already bypassed the Harbor property, leaving in its wake small, unprofitable loft buildings that were often surrendered by the lessees to the trust. A real estate adviser to the trustees wrote in 1896, "It is almost pitiful to go through Eighth Street and see the fronts coming down out of old buildings and cheap fronts taking their places, while the class of business going into the street is of a cheap and poor order." Ninth Street was described as "dreary."

Henry George and the Randall Farm

Whatever their shortcomings in the matter of leases, the trustees could be forgiven for failing to see that they would be a factor in the 1886 mayoral election that historian Allan Nevins was to call "the most stirring campaign in the city's history." Tammany had nominated Democrat Abram Hewitt, millionaire son-in-law of Peter Cooper and a veteran congressman. Young Theodore Roosevelt was the Republican candidate. The candidate who caused the stir, however, was Henry George, the single-tax reformer who was running as the Central Labor Union's candidate. George contended in his *Progress and Poverty*—which had been translated into French, German, Russian, Chinese, and a half-dozen other languages—that renting land is robbery that profits a few individuals rather than the community whose existence made the property valuable.[2] The Randall farm was a favorite example of villainy. It produced great wealth, the argument went, not through any efforts of the Harbor trustees but because of the growth of the city. Had the leaseholders' rents and taxes flowed into a public purse, "it would have been easy to make New York the most delightful place of residence." Hewitt won the election in a close race over George. Roosevelt was a distant third.

Single-tax advocate Henry George, running for mayor in 1886, targeted the Randall farm as an example of real estate villainy.

William Rhinelander Stewart of the Rhinelander Mansion, Washington Square North and Fifth Avenue, raised funds for a temporary arch to commemorate the centennial of Washington's presidential inauguration.

Washington Square in Transition

Change enveloped Washington Square as well as Broadway. As early as the 1850s, the streets south and west of the square began to decline. Tenements replaced Federal row houses when the tide of Irish, German, and Italian immigrants dislodged the gentry from what had been known as the American Ward.

New York University (NYU) all but abandoned the square in the 1890s in favor of its new University Heights campus in the Bronx. In 1894, the rundown University Building was demolished. Alfred Zucker, architect of many loft buildings in the university area and near Houston Street, was hired by the university to design a classically styled, 10-story commercial structure. The American Book Company rented the first seven floors, while the top three floors housed the university's professional schools of law and pedagogy. Gothic Revival disappeared entirely from the square in 1895 when the South Dutch Reformed Church was razed and replaced by the 10-story Celluloid Building. Since 1927, NYU has occupied all floors of what is now known as Main Building. Beginning in the 1960s, NYU took over most of the commercial buildings in the neighborhood of the square, 21 in a recent count, and adapted them for a variety of university uses.

On Washington Square North, the mansion at number 20 was converted in 1880 into apartments by architect Henry Hardenberg, who designed the Dakota and the Plaza Hotel. Number 3, site of the New York Foundling Hospital from 1870 to 1873, was transformed into five stories of Victorian flats for artists in 1884 by owner-architect Robert Terhune. Fifty-five years would pass before another significant architectural change was made on the uptown side of the park.

Bourgeois and Bohemian

The northern border of Washington Square and the lower portion of Fifth Avenue continued to be home to families of social standing who agreed with Henry James's observation: "This portion of New York appears to many persons the most delectable. It has a kind of established repose which is not of frequent occurrence in other quarters of the long, shrill city; it has a riper, richer, more honorable look than any of the upper ramifications of the great longitudinal thoroughfare—the look of having something of a social history."[3]

Fifth Avenue resident and architectural critic Marianna Griswold Van Rensselaer wrote in 1893, "A belief was gaining ground that, whatever may happen a little further up the avenue, this quarter-mile stretch will remain a good residence neighborhood. The local residents are proud of the aroma of 50 years antiquity which we breathe, and we delight to maintain that this is the only part of New York, outside of the tenement districts, where a neighborhood feeling exists."[4]

In a letter to the trustees of Sailors' Snug Harbor, Robert W. de Forest, president of the Metropolitan Museum of Art, wrote about "my own desire to have my family continue in its present home because that home was built by Mrs. de Forest's grandfather and in it she was born.... [and] my desire as a citizen to preserve some part of old New York."[5] With new leases due in 1894, de Forest reminded the board that he and his neighbors needed to be assured of future rentals on a fair basis. An annual lease of $1,050 was agreed upon. The de Forests lived at 7 Washington Square North until just before World War II.

In 1889, William Rhinelander Stewart of 17 Washington Square North collected $2,765 from friends and neighbors to raise a triumphal wood and plaster arch near the Fifth Avenue entrance to the square to commemorate the centennial of George Washington's inauguration as the nation's first president. Stanford White was commissioned to design it. The arch was so popular that White was called upon again, this time to perpetuate his work in the marble version that stands there today.[6]

As Caroline Ware pointed out in *Greenwich Village: 1920-1930*, families such as the Van Rensselaers, de Forests, and Rhinelander-Stewarts made up a nucleus similar to that of Beacon Hill in Boston or Rittenhouse Square in Philadelphia, around which a reclaimed residential district could be developed more easily than in a section that had become wholly devoted to business.[7]

The Washington Square neighborhood developed a second and unique nucleus—the artists and writers who turned Greenwich Village into a bohemian mecca in the years before the first World War. These rebels against Victorianism found tolerance—or indifference—among a population of immigrant adherents of the Vatican and Tammany Hall, "garlic and dago red," in the terminology of the times. Not all the dissenters had come to the Village for cheap rents.

The most famous address in prewar times was 23 Fifth Avenue on the northeast corner of Ninth Street. Here, in a smartly decorated, second-floor apartment that had been sublet from Gettysburg hero General Dan Sickles, Mabel Dodge—a rich divorcee who descended on New York following a decade of high living in Europe—conducted her celebrated "evenings," beginning in January 1913. As Lincoln Steffens recalled, "poor and rich, labor skates and scabs, painters, musicians, reporters, editors, swells" clinked whiskey glasses and debated the issues of the day—Freud, Marx, Picasso, and free love. Although Dodge was adroit hostess rather than artist or intellectual, her Wednesday evenings were incubators for two controversial and historically important extravaganzas in 1913. The Sixty-Ninth Regiment Armory Show in February introduced both the cultured and curious to the then radical art styles of Cézanne, Van Gogh, Matisse, Duchamp, Picasso, and scores of other avant-garde artists. Four months later, before 15,000 spectators in Madison Square Garden, an International Workers of the World Pageant dramatized the plight of thousands of strikers at silk mills in Paterson, New Jersey. Although the strike collapsed within a month, the pageant was an inspiration for much of the experimental theater that was to bloom in Greenwich Village for years to come.

The 1913 International Exhibition of Modern Art at the Armory and the Paterson Strike Pageant had a single incubator—Mabel Dodge's provocative "Evenings."

When her lover, newspaperman John Reed, went to Mexico in 1916 to cover Pancho Villa, then to Russia to report on the Bolshevik seizure of power, Dodge closed her fabled salon and soon moved to New Mexico. The evenings had lasted less than three years, but they were a spicy ingredient in the radicalism and naughtiness that were rapidly creating an international aura for the blocks around Washington and Sheridan Squares.

By the 1890s, the decaying row houses on the south side of the square had become cheap cafes and inexpensive boarding houses that were to feed and shelter a colony of writers, artists, and social activists marching in favor of any cause that was taboo in the Middle West. Number 61, "the house of genius," was home at one time or another to writers Stephen Crane, O. Henry, Frank Norris, Maxwell Bodenheim, satirist Gelect Burgess ("I Never Saw a Purple Cow"), and poet Alan Seegar who was to keep his "Rendezvous

*Washington Mews.
Stables behind the
Washington Square
mansions became stu-
dios for artists and
writers when automo-
biles made them
cheaply available
for men rather than
horses.*

with Death" in 1916 on a battlefield in France. Soprano Adelina Patti lived at number 61 before making it to the stage of the Metropolitan Opera, and on the top floor Rose O'Neil invented the Kewpie doll. Neighborhood lore added Eugene O'Neill, Theodore Dreiser, and John Dos Passos to 61's roster. Other tenants on that same south-side block included writers Willa Cather, John Reed, Lincoln Steffens, and artist Maurice Prendergast.

The rows of stables behind the mansions on Washington Square became studios when automobiles made these quarters cheaply available for men instead of horses. MacDougal Alley became the workplace for painters Ernest Lawson and Guy Pene du Bois; sculptor Jo Davidson; and three-time winner of the Pulitzer Prize for poetry Edwin Arlington Robinson. Gertrude Vanderbilt Whitney founded the Whitney Museum at 17 MacDougal Alley. Washington Mews was home to political columnist Walter Lippman; Edward Bernays, nephew of Sigmund Freud and the pioneer press agent who put orange juice on the American breakfast table; and Grover Whalen, the city's official greeter for more than half a century. Edward Hopper, Rockwell Kent, and Walter Pach were among the many artists who had studios in number 3, the converted house in "The Row." It was there that John Sloan and William Glackens sowed the seeds that bloomed as the Ashcan School of Art, and John Dos Passos wrote *Manhattan Transfer*.

Fires and a Subway

Politicians and industrialists had ignored an epidemic of warehouse fires in Hell's Hundred Acres, now the SoHo district (SOuth of HOuston Street). That complacency ended in tragedy when 146 young women, working as seamstresses for the Triangle Shirtwaist Company in the 10-story Asch Building, perished in a fire on Saturday afternoon March 21, 1911. More than 500 women, mostly Jewish and Italian, labored for $3 a 52-hour week sewing the lightweight blouses depicted as the uniform of modern womanhood in the illustrations of Charles Dana Gibson. Sidewalks on Washington Place and Greene Street were converted into a makeshift morgue for the charred bodies of the victims. Many, finding exit doors bolted by management, had leaped from the ninth floor. Now owned by NYU and known as the Brown Building, the 1900 structure houses the university's biology and chemistry departments. A bronze

More than 500 young seamstresses were trapped in the Triangle Shirtwaist Company fire on a Saturday afternoon in March 1911.

plaque at the corner of the building commemorates the needlessly lost lives.

Not only did the resulting outrage inspire enactment of the nation's most stringent fire laws and building codes, it brought Village activists to the barricades to rally and demonstrate in favor of unionization, votes for women, a ban against sweatshops, and whatever else was likely to make the neighborhood uncomfortable for laissez-faire employers.

At least as important as the activists' ire in the Village's return from commercial to residential quarter was the city's 1913 approval of a subway route to be constructed under Seventh Avenue, a realtor's dream-come-true that would turn a

The Brevoort Hotel, on Fifth Avenue at Eighth Street, offered Parisian-flavored cafe life.

backwater into a convenient place to live—halfway between the financial district and the shopping and entertainment centers.

Harbor trustees had alertly seen the transition coming for more than a decade. In 1902, board president Morris K. Jesup had called for "radical changes in our system of leasing" to provide larger plots with longer terms and reasonable rents. In addition, Jesup suggested, and the board agreed, that "we set aside annually from our income a certain amount which shall be known as the repair and building fund." Excellent as the plan was, Jesup had to admit that "it demands much larger sums of money than the Board has any immediate prospect of finding."

John Wanamaker was about to help fill the income gap. The master merchant from Philadelphia had taken over the old A. T. Stewart leases in 1896. Within a half-dozen years, he needed much more space. A crafty deal maker, Wanamaker threatened to move uptown unless the Harbor met his terms. Jesup found him so difficult that he gave up and called upon Alexander E. Orr, his predecessor as president of the trustees and the chamber of commerce, to take over the negotiations. Orr, a realtor, was also chairman of the Rapid Transit Commission and a tough bargainer. Following innumerable meetings and rejected propositions, Orr told Wanamaker, "Before you leave this office, either accept or reject; otherwise I will notify the Harbor Trustees that I have failed to arrive at a settlement and recommend that they call everything off and fall back on their rights under existing leases as they mature." Wanamaker gave in, and a leasehold for the square block south of the Stewart Building between Eighth and Ninth Streets was signed on May 1, 1903.

The annex, completed in 1907, was far larger than the six-story main store. Its 14 floors plus basement with an entrance to the new Fourth Avenue subway contained almost as much space as the Empire State Building would when it opened in 1931.[9] Wanamaker's annual rent on his two block fronts was approximately $1.1 million on a lease of 84 years.

John Wanamaker, master merchant and crafty deal maker.

The plan to upgrade Harbor properties got under way in 1916 with the remodeling of a row of houses at 4 to 26 East Eighth Street. The work, described in chapter 4, gave a colorful lift to a block in decline. In 1918, a similar row from 4 to 18 East Ninth Street was remodeled. The improvement campaign shifted into higher gear in 1922 when a nondescript, four-story building and one-story shack on the northeast corner of Ninth and University Place were replaced by a handsome, 11-story apartment building that contained 24 sizable suites.

In 1925, the trustees teamed up with the architectural firm of Helme and Corbett and the apartment-house specialists Sugarman and Berger to construct a 27-story apartment hotel between Washington Mews and Eighth Street that would be known as 1 Fifth Avenue. "1/5" was a sensation. First, no one had attempted to build a skyscraper tower in the area between Fourteenth and Canal Streets because of sandy subsoil. Second, the building was stunningly handsome with a set-back, art deco profile that has been a visual landmark in the city to this day. The venture's success quelled some of the complaints about the loss of the four fine townhouses that had occupied the site.

In the mid-1920s, the trustees sold 47 little-used southern acres of their Staten Island property for $335,550 to builders who developed a community of suburban homes and garden apartments that is known as Randall Manor. Profits from the sale helped finance three more stylish apartment houses at 35 and 45 East Ninth Street and 40–50 East Tenth. Heat for the new buildings was produced in the furnace room of 40–50 and distributed through a tunnel network that remained in use until the 1950s when the apartment houses became separate cooperatives. 40–50 East Tenth, which opened in early 1929, was actually three connected buildings with individual entrances and three elevator banks that offered—as they still do—joint access only on the top, lobby, and base-ment floors. These were expansive residences for the upper-middle class with doormen, living-room fireplaces, foyers, one or two bedrooms, at least 1-1/2 baths, and dining rooms in many suites. Annual rents were, to modern tenants, surprisingly modest, ranging from $1,700 to $2,100. Another $100 a year paid for a maid's room on the tenth floor. In 1990, one of the co-ops sold for $1 million.

Aside from the 1939 remodeling that turned seven buildings in The Row on Washington Square North into a modern apartment house with a Greek Revival facade, the Harbor's ambitious rebuilding program was forced into a 15-year hiatus by the Great Depression and World War II.

Rehabilitation costs had totaled more than $3 million, according to the Harbor comptroller, W. A. Guenther, in a letter to the Central Hanover Bank and Trust Company in August 1936. He reported that the expenses were paid from the Harbor's annual income, which greatly reduced main-tenance on the Staten Island property. In an unpublished article written by one of its officers, the bank said: "The action of the Trustees was undoubtedly wise and far-sighted as a means of extricating the institution from what might have been a very serious situation. In spite of the added handicaps of the depression, it appears only a matter of time when the greater part of the Manhattan holdings will be bringing in a satisfactory and stable income."

By 1947, the Manhattan real estate market had returned to vigorous life. The Harbor's opening postwar move was to lease to NYU for 200 years, with options to renew, the square block bounded by Washington Square North, Fifth Avenue, University Place, and Eighth Street, with the exception of 1 Fifth Avenue and the adjoining property at 4 Eighth Street. Along with store space, the leased property contained 190 apartments with 530 rooms, a few of which NYU already held on lease.

Speaking at an April 1949 press conference called to announce the long-rumored deal, NYU Chancellor Harry Woodburn Chase pledged,

"Occupants of the properties involved will not be disturbed; nor is there any intention to alter the character of the buildings facing Washington Square." Chase was obviously speaking in response to a citizens' rally called "to prevent the destruction of the Square."

Theodore Sicama, Harbor comptroller, noted that the trustees had turned down many offers by large apartment-house interests for the property leased to NYU. The lease, he added, would facilitate Harbor plans to develop attractive buildings "of modest height and architectural unity that will include studio apartments at reasonable rentals."

Fourteen months later, the trustees agreed to lease the block enclosed by University Place, Broadway, and Eighth and Ninth Streets to a developer for 99 years. Approximately 50 small structures, considered "obsolete and unsightly" by the trustees, would be replaced by buildings designed to house nearly 1,200 families. Sailors' Snug Harbor was to receive $1,742,000 in annual net rentals for the first 21 years. From then on, yearly payments would be based on 5 percent of the value of the land, but not less than $125,000.

The largest of the new complexes, 40 East Ninth, is a tan-brick setback with balconies standing 12 stories above a raised garden terrace and underground garage. Impresario Joseph Papp, founder of the Shakespeare Festival and The Public Theater in what had been the Astor Library, lived there for 18 years. Its neighbors at 30 and 60 East Ninth are each drab, red-brick, six-story buildings distinguished only by their names, The Lafayette and The Hamilton. Main entrances to all three are on Ninth Street. On Eighth Street, the trio present a lineup of 23 shops that deliver a variety of services—barber, florist, optician, mailbox rental—and offer barbecue and sushi, pizza and frozen custard, housewares and greeting cards, plus a bicycle shop and four boutiques with women's wear. The Broadway block included a Woolworth and a drugstore, while University Place featured a supermarket, a fancy dry cleaner, and the Knickerbocker, a neighborhood favorite for food and jazz.

40 East Ninth Street, home to impresario Joseph Papp from 1973 to 1991, was one of three apartment houses that replaced 50 small buildings on Harbor land in the early 1950s.

The Knickerbocker occupies hallowed ground. From 1883, as the Hotel Martin, and from 1902 until 1949 as the Lafayette, this site attracted Villagers and notables from the art and literary worlds who came here to experience Parisian-flavored cafe life. Only the nearby Brevoort

Hotel and its basement cafe, which extended to the Fifth Avenue sidewalk in warm weather, could inspire similar affection from a clientele of the dissident and the opulent. Cobbled together from three brownstones in 1854, the Brevoort maintained, along with its cafe, a celebrated dining room where Americans were introduced to escargots and frogs' legs Provençal. The hotel also served as a leisurely meeting place for a number of organizations including the trustees of Sailors' Snug Harbor, who gathered there for lunch monthly from 1920 until 1952 when it was razed for a luxury apartment house called the Brevoort. Both the Lafayette and the Brevoort had been owned and managed since 1902 by Paris-born Raymond Orteig. It was he who put up the $25,000 prize won in 1927 by Charles Lindbergh for completing the first nonstop, solo flight from New York to Paris. Orteig and Orville Wright presented the prize money to Lindbergh at the Brevoort on June 16, three days after 4 million cheering people welcomed Lindbergh home with a ticker-tape parade from the Battery up Broadway and Fifth Avenue to Central Park.

The restaurateur had planned to present the prize money at a well-advertised breakfast, but Lindbergh's schedule said otherwise. His day began in Brooklyn with another massive parade, followed by a ceremonial visit to Roosevelt Field where the historic flight began. Next he was rushed to the Bronx, where Yankee fans had been promised a visit. But Lindbergh had time only to be driven up to the stadium before rushing downtown to the Brevoort for a 6 P.M. presentation. He spoke briefly, noting that Orteig's offer had inspired him to enter the race, for it was "nothing more nor less a challenge to pilots and engineers in aeronautics to see whether they could build and fly a plane from New York to Paris. I don't believe any such challenge, within reason, will go unanswered." That said, Lindbergh was off to a reception and banquet with the Aeronautical Chamber of Commerce. The evening ended with a party given by William Randolph Hearst in his West Side home. The next morning, the young hero flew the *Spirit of St. Louis* to its namesake city.[10]

Another famed hangout on Harbor land—the Cedar Street Tavern—fell in the 1960s when the eastern extension of the Brevoort apartment complex took over the west side of University Place between Eighth and Ninth Streets. Unlike Orteig's cafes, the tavern gloried in blue-collar chic. Here the young giants of abstract expressionism—among them Jackson Pollack, William de Kooning, Franz Kline, and Larry Rivers—discussed, with an occasional exchange of punches, the work that was making New

York, rather than Paris, the center of modern art. In the 1950s, the artists were joined by another sometimes-belligerent group, the Beat writers and poets, Jack Kerouac, Allen Ginsberg, Frank O'Hara, Le Roi Jones, and Kenneth Koch.

By the 1960s Sicama's promise about modest heights and reasonable rents should have been an embarrassment. The buff-colored Brevoort covered an entire square block with 14 stories that included a series of five setback penthouse floors. By the mid-1990s, one-bedroom, one-bath condominiums sold for $350,000. Randall House, on the site of the colonial mansion Minto, rose 14 uninspired red-brick floors on Broadway between Ninth and Tenth Streets. Georgetown Plaza, a banal 31-floor tower on Broadway between Waverly Place and Eighth, was a favorite target of architectural as well as preservationist critics in part because its size broke the continuity of height and character of Broadway's traditional street wall.

Wanamaker had closed its Village department-store operation in 1954. The giant southern building was restructured for office space. K-Mart brought the department store back to the neighborhood in 1996 when it leased three floors and basement space in the former Wanamaker's South

While awaiting the wrecker's ball, the grand old A. T. Stewart store took fiery leave of Broadway in a raging blaze that burned out of control for two days in July 1956. Standing in its place since 1960 is the 22-story Stewart House, the first apartments built as a cooperative in the Village.

By the early 1960s, 225 leased building lots had been consolidated into 18. A total of 10 skyscraper apartment buildings with 2,445 housing units had been built on Sailors' Snug Harbor property between 1951 and 1966. Back in 1930, the trustees had hired a consulting architect to advise them on their "property improvement" program. They chose one of the most distinguished American city planners, George B. Ford, general director of the Regional Plan Association and recipient of the French Legion of Honor for his work in rebuilding the devastated cities of France following World War I. Within a month of signing on with the Harbor, Ford died unexpectedly at age 51. With Ford's death and the depression, the trustees abandoned their effort to rationalize their rebuilding plans. It may have been just as well. In his *New York 1960*, architect and critic Robert A. M. Stern noted that the Harbor's "preference for numerous individual leases led to piecemeal demolition and rebuilding of its properties—ensuring at least a small measure of urbanistic and architectural variety. . . . The damage they wrought to the Village's traditional idiosyncrasy was minor compared to the bold plans that Robert Moses, in his capacity as chairman of the Mayor's Committee on Slum Clearance, announced in January 1951."

By the 1950s, the tenants who filled these new apartments were more likely to be young brokers and editors attracted by the artistic cachet and off-beat charm of the Village than the bohemians of the past. A *Partisan Review* article in 1954, headlined, "The Village: Bohemia Gone Bourgeois," bemoaned the fundamentally conventional tastes of the new-comers. "She's from Vassar, he's in advertising, they like African masks, Swedish furniture." True enough. But the Village, in a state of change and renewal for nearly all the twentieth century, remains tolerant, liberal, diverse, and a genteel place to live.

Notes

1. Hone's quote in Allan Nevins's edition of the *Diary* is reported in Edmund Delaney's *Greenwich Village*, p. 34.

2. Henry George's theory about the trustees and the Randall farm was explained by the Land and Labor Library's W.T. Crosdale in an 1887 article.

3. See *The American Scene*, Henry James's 1907 account of a native's return to New York.

4. The Griswold Van Rensselar article is quoted in Robert A. M. Stern, *New York 1900*, p. 18.

5. The deForest letter is located in Harbor archives.

6. Rhinelander Stewart's collection for the arch is reported by Mindy Cantor in *Greenwich Village: Culture and Counterculture*, ed. Rick Beard and Leslie Cohen Berlowitz, pp. 83-4.

7. Caroline F. Ware, *Greenwich Village 1920-1930*, p. 17.

8. For Mabel Dodge, see Martin Green, *New York 1913: The Armory Show and the Paterson Strike Pageant.*

9. Elliot Willensky and Norval White, *AIA Guide to New York City*, p. 156.

10. See A. Scott Berg's *Lindbergh* for an account of Lindbergh's frenetic visit to New York and his acceptance of the Orteig prize, pp. 152-9.

Depression and War

A year before the Great Depression caught everyone's attention on Black Tuesday, October 29, 1929, seamen's welfare agencies were reporting growing numbers of unemployed merchant mariners.[1] Before long, Federal Reserve indexes of industry faltered; inventories mounted; and factory payrolls, freight-car loadings, and department-store sales declined. Agriculture was distressed. All these cracks in the economy were hidden by curtains of optimism stitched together through three years of booming business and soaring stock prices.

Months after the Crash sent the economy spinning into doldrums that would not lift until the nation began to rearm in 1939, business and administration leaders were looking for a quick reversal. The National Association of Manufacturers covered billboards with a cartoon of Miss Columbia promising, "Business Is Good. Keep It Good. Nothing Can Stop US." President Herbert Hoover announced on May 1, 1930, "We have now passed the worst."[2]

Fortunes were wiped out, including millions of savings accounts. By the summer of 1932, the Dow Jones Industrials were worth one-tenth of what they had been worth three years earlier. A quarter of the American

If this well-dressed peddler sold all his apples and tangerines, he earned $1.85 for his day's work.

workforce was unemployed. Many of those who still had jobs worked only two or three days a week. Nearly 20 percent of New York's population received public assistance of some kind. A vast emergency shelter on the East River docks housed thousands of men overnight. The Great Lawn in Central Park was filled with cardboard shacks sheltering the homeless in what was known as a "Hooverville." An oft-photographed scene of the time showed hollow-cheeked men selling apples on street corners. Peddlers paid $1.75 a crate, sold each apple for a nickel, and pocketed a profit of about $1.85 for a day's work, providing that all the apples had been sold.[3]

Living was tough for almost everyone, and among the hardest hit were merchant sailors. Several thousand seamen were in port on any given day. In normal times of seasonal unemployment, the adaptable mariner might fill in as a painter or carpenter, janitor or apartment-house handyman while waiting for shipping to improve. Now the best a jobless seaman could do was register for help at a desk set up at South Ferry by the Seaman's Section of the Welfare Council. The Seamens' Church Institute of New York estimated that no more than 2 or 3 percent could find berths of any kind. The rest were "on the beach."

The Joint Emergency Committee of Seamen's Welfare Agencies estimated in November 1931 that at least 1,000 beds and $100,000 would be needed to care for destitute mariners during the coming winter. The Salvation Army and other agencies that had been spending money of their own to aid out-of-work sailors needed government help to carry on the good work. They could not get it. An $18 million crisis fund provided by the city was limited to heads of family and metropolitan-area residents. Few seamen qualified. The Department of Public Health turned down a request for a South Ferry pier where nearly 1,000 seamen could be sheltered because that would be unfair to other trades. The State Temporary Relief Administration ignored a call for help on the grounds that merchant seamen came under federal rule. However, Washington said that this was not so.[4]

Private companies still in business and the hard-up public finally came to the rescue. A campaign by the Joint Emergency Committee to raise funds to feed and shelter seamen brought in $28,000 in two weeks. By June 1932, the committee had provided 147,500 nights of lodging and twice that number of meals with $102,000 in subscriptions. The good news was accompanied by a committee estimate that the number of mariners needing assistance in the coming year would increase by 50 percent.

A unique source of aid was suggested in Hearst's daily *American* by columnist Harry Acton: Charge the happy folks attending bon voyage parties on the luxury liners docked at the Hudson River's famed Steamship Row 10 cents each to come aboard. The steamship companies agreed; foreign vessels sent half the boarding fees home to help their own distressed sailors. Thousands of seamen benefited from the boarding fund through the remaining years of the depression.[5]

Shipboard parties seem out of context with the times, but they underline an often overlooked point about the depression—not everyone was flat broke. And, whatever money one had bought more because of deflation. Many of the formerly rich moved out of townhouses and Park Avenue apartments and into suddenly chic walkups on East Side streets.[6] *House and Garden* reported in 1933 that these new tenement tenants were "living gallantly in simplicity and liking it."

Park Avenue's Waldorf-Astoria Hotel and the Empire State Building opened in 1931, followed a year later by the first of the Rockefeller Center buildings. Three of the city's most glamorous night spots—the Stork Club, El Morocco, and Jack and Charlie's "21" Club—came into the open with the end of Prohibition in 1933. The unmatchable Rainbow Room opened on the sixty-fifth floor of the RCA Building in 1934.

Serious aid for the less fortunate arrived with the New Deal and passage of the Federal Emergency Relief Act of 1933 followed by a ruling

The Hudson River's Steamship Row, which ran from 44th to 57th Street. In the 1930s, guests at bon voyage parties were each charged a dime to board the luxury liners that docked here. The admission fee benefited unemployed seamen.

that seamen came under the heading of transients. As such, Washington was responsible for them. Like the Indians, mariners joked, they now were wards of the federal government. The government arranged with a number of agencies to provide three meals a day and shelter at 55 cents an individual. The fee was supplemented with large donations of meat, eggs, and butter.

Surviving at Sailors' Snug Harbor

When the Joint Emergency Committee of Seamen's Welfare Agencies called upon the Harbor for help, the trustees sent a check for $1,000 and word that there was no room for any destitute sailors needing shelter during the approaching winter. For only the second time in its history, the Harbor had to turn away eligible applicants. (In post–Civil War years, the home had been filled to its 400-bed capacity.) The minimum age limit for admission was raised from 60 to 65. To make room for more deep-sea sailors, the Harbor limited the number of offshore fishermen to 150 and suspended the eligibility of Great Lakes mariners. Staff salaries and trustee fees were reduced by 10 percent.

As many as 926 men had been housed at the beginning of the twentieth century. With population beginning to decline in the 1920s, Harbor officials had cut capacity to 875 when they turned over a small dormitory to the staff. By squeezing as many as five men into some of the larger two-occupant rooms in 1930, the population expanded to 900.

Quarters were cramped at times but, with little doubt, residents of the Harbor were the most serene seamen in the port of New York during the years of the depression. Trustees, on the other hand, continually grappled with severe fiscal problems. Even when maintenance needs were ignored, income barely covered expenses.

Tenants appealed for rent reductions because of curtailed income. Raymond Orteig warned that his Hotel Brevoort was "a losing venture beyond all hope of redemption" unless Harbor trustees rescinded his recent rent increase. They did. They granted rent concessions to scores of apartment tenants "for the purpose of tiding them over a temporary situation." Uncollectable rents for the year 1934 already totaled $28,505 by February 9. One-year lease renewals "at the best prices obtainable" were offered to 44 factory-loft lessees. Many such leases were surrendered, usually leaving the trustees to pay the taxes on old, economically obsolete, and badly deteriorating buildings.

Depression troubles were reflected in the decision to cancel a planned celebration on August 1, 1933, commemorating the centennial of the opening of Sailors' Snug Harbor on Staten Island. Back in 1902, the hundredth anniversary of the actual founding had been marked with a double celebration. On that Sunday afternoon of May 28, at the Randall Memorial Church, "a musical service" was held, featuring six soloists and a chorus of 60 voices. On Wednesday more than 2,000 celebrants—about half with invitations printed by Tiffany—were present for a champagne luncheon served in tents on the great lawn. Eight hundred arrived from Manhattan on a steamer hired for the day. Officers from the Brooklyn Navy Yard were ferried on a tug. Visitors toured the flag-bedecked buildings, and listened to an organ recital in the Randall Memorial and to the Mount Loretto Boys Band. Vaudeville acts entertained them on the lawn next to the governor's mansion.

Bad as the Harbor's situation was in 1933, it hardly compared in severity with that facing New York City's other famous philanthropic landlord, Trinity Church. Thanks to Queen Anne's 1704 gift of 215 acres of undeveloped land that would eventually become the west side of lower Manhattan, Trinity had a patrimony almost 10 times the size of that left by Randall. Through three centuries, the Episcopal parish at the head of Wall Street gave away more than $56 million in gifts, allowances, and grants including the original site of what was to become Columbia University and the land for several of New York's downtown streets. Despite this unmatched display of almsgiving, Trinity was still a major player in the Manhattan real estate market at the time of the Crash. When more and more of its commercial tenants and building owners found it impossible to pay rent, mortgages, and real estate taxes, Trinity was forced to assume debts and titles to buildings operating at a deficit. Trinity stood on the brink of bankruptcy for 10 years with a debt of more than $24 million. A mortgage loan of $7.2 million arranged by its vestry in 1936 carried the church through to the war years, when the debt began to diminish.[7]

Getting Out the Vote, Finally

State Supreme Court Justice William J. Gaynor, later a noteworthy mayor of New York City, disenfranchised the residents of Sailors' Snug Harbor by ruling in 1904 that "inmates of charitable institutions" had no right to vote in governmental elections.[8] Most of the seamen, voracious newspaper readers, continued to take an indignant but now inactive interest in politics.

With the approach of the November 1932 election between Herbert

Hoover and Franklin Roosevelt, a group of the old sailors won an appeal against the 1904 ruling. By October, 245 had registered to vote and a straw poll showed the residents favoring Roosevelt 334 to 14. On Republican appeal, the seamen's new voting privilege was withdrawn before the election. The issue was eventually settled in the seamen's favor. Finally, in 1936, with full citizenship rights restored for the first time in 32 years, Harbor residents were free to cast their votes for Roosevelt or for the GOP's Alfred Landon, or William Lemke, candidate of Father Charles Coughlin's new Union Party, or the White Supremacy ticket's Eugene Talmadge, or Socialist Party candidate Norman Thomas, or the Communist Party's Earl Browder, or the Prohibitionist candidate whoever he or she may have been.

World War II

Many healthy residents of the Harbor had declared through the years that they would leave their comfortable home on Staten Island tomorrow if only a ship could be found to take them on again. But there were no berths for old-timers.

Pearl Harbor changed that. In the months following the Japanese attack on December 7, 1941, Captain Charles Nelson, 70, signed on as third officer on an army transport as did Herbert L. Redmond and Carl G. Muller, both in their late 60s. George W. Dunn, 71, shipped out as an assistant engineer. John Mathieson joined the crew of a merchantman. Seventeen others found ship berths or jobs in the Brooklyn Navy Yard where some 5,000 vessels were built or repaired during the war. Twenty-five resident volunteers were rejected for physical reasons.[9]

On December 14, 1941, Company F of the 61st Coast Artillery set up its anti-aircraft guns on the fringes of Harbor property. With permission from Harbor Governor Howard A. Flynn, enlisted men were quartered in basement rooms of Building H, adjoining the mess hall. Five officers shared a room in the administration building. Flynn reported to the trustees that the soldiers "caused no conflicts with normal operations."

What the navy had in mind for the Harbor would have been totally disruptive. In October, the trustees were told that the entire institution might be leased as a training center. The board was less than enthusiastic. Speculation about finding new quarters for the retirees ended happily in December when the navy decided that the Harbor did not have enough classroom space to meet its needs.

Harbor residents watched from front-row seats the transformation of the port into a maritime citadel of war beginning early in 1940. German U-boats kept France's *Ile de France* and *Normandie*, Britain's *Queen Mary* and *Aquitania*, and Italy's *Rex* moored to their Hudson River piers off Manhattan's West Fifties while they were refitted for missions of war. The *Queen Elizabeth*, already in military gray, slid into her Pier 90 berth across from the *Mary* on March 6. Recently launched, she had been in the fitting-out basin at Clydeside when war broke out in September 1939. Her maiden voyage was a secret, zigzag, five-day, 19-hour race to New York. She remained at Pier 90 until November. Each of the Queens carried 16,000 GIs per voyage to Europe and Africa in what was a continuous ferry service throughout the war.[10]

The *Ile de France* spent eight months at a municipal pier in Tompkinsville, Staten Island, before sailing one midnight for England with a cargo of war material. The *Normandie*, acquisitioned by the U.S. Navy after the fall of France and rechristened *U.S.S. Lafayette*, was slated to become a troop carrier. What follows is a postwar report from the French Line:

> At 2:35 P.M. on February 9, 1942, a workman's blowtorch set fire to the first-class lounge. There was no extinguisher nearby. The fire bucket was accidentally knocked over. The doors to the promenade deck were open, and a strong Northwester fanned the flames. The U.S. Coastguard on duty on the bridge could not find the button for the alarm klaxons. The automatic fire alarm linking the ship with the New York Fire Department had been disconnected on January 13. . . . Nobody knew how to shut the fireproof bulkhead that isolated the lounge, or how to work the hose reels. The American couplings did not fit the French couplings of the fire main. . . . At around 8 P.M. the Fire Department announced that the fire had been brought under control . . . but the ship was not saved. Under the weight of the tons of water that had built up in her tanks, the *Normandie* began to list. In an hour the list reached 20 degrees. By 11 P.M. it was 40 degrees. . . . At 2:45 A.M., ship's time, the flagship of the French Line heeled over 80 degrees to port, between Pier 88 and Pier 90. The *Normandie* was no more.[11]

One of the earliest of convoys that assembled in and sailed from the port consisted of six freighters dispatched from England following the

A blacked-out Broadway during wartime.

evacuation of the defeated British and French armies from Dunkirk in May and June 1940. Left behind on the beaches were tens of thousands of rifles, artillery pieces, vehicles, and 7,000 tons of ammunition. In response to a plea for help from Winston Churchill, American arsenals were all but stripped of guns and ammunition for shipment by the trainload to the waiting freighters.

For the port of New York, the war's worst phase began on January 13, 1942, when Admiral Karl Doenitz, commander in chief of the German navy, ordered his submarine wolf packs from the North Atlantic to the East Coast from Cape Cod to the Caribbean. Hunting thrived off Ambrose Light, where 50 ships entered or left New York harbor via Sandy Hook Channel every 24 hours. Neither navy nor civilians were prepared for the onslaught. Now that the United States was officially at war, destroyers escorted convoys all the way across the Atlantic. Few were assigned to coastal duty, however. And, fewer than 100 planes patrolled some 3,000 miles of coastal water. Because the coastline was not completely blacked out for weeks, German U-boats could see silhouettes of unarmed tankers and freighters against the glow of city lights. By the time the coordinated U-boat attacks ended in June 1942, more than 400 ships had been sunk and several thousand merchant seamen killed.[12]

The worst was over. Scores of newly built, small, escort vessels and converted yachts formed a coastal convoy system while the navy developed more efficient means of tracking submarines so that they could be sunk by big Liberator bombers and destroyers with depth charges. In the second half of 1942, coastal convoys lost only half of one percent of their ships.

On any spring day in 1943, there was likely to be in the North Atlantic 31 convoys with nearly 700 merchant ships and 145 escorts. All but about 1 percent would make the voyage safely. New York was the principal assembly point. For days, vessels would arrive and anchor in the Upper Bay. The day after they sailed, the port looked empty. But not for long, as the old seamen who kept track of such things knew.

Notes

1. James C. Healey's *Foc's'le and Glory Hole* provides depressing details and statistics about the seamen's situation. Also see the Federal Writers Project, *New York Panorama.*

2. The National Association of Manufacturers billboards and Hoover's remarks are found in Samuel Eliot Morison, *Oxford History of the American People*, p. 945.

3. Arithmetic for apple sellers appears in Thomas Kessner, *Fiorello H. La Guardia*, p. 168.

4. See Healey, *Foc's'le and Glory Hole*; and Federal Writers Project, *New York Panorama.*

5. Harry Acton's column is reported by Healey, p. 145.

6. The suddenly chic walkups were recalled by Christopher Gray, *New York Times*, "Streetscapes," December 14, 1997.

7. Trinity's gifts and problems are discussed in Gerald J. Barry, *Trinity Church: 300 Years of Philanthropy.*

8. Disenfranchisement was discussed in an article about the Harbor in the October 1, 1933, *New Yorker.*

9. Several articles about the elderly volunteers appeared in the *Staten Island Advance.*

10. The wartime appearance of the port is described in the Federal Writers Project, *A Maritime History of New York.*

11. See Christian Cleres's history of the French line, *Le Havre-New York*, pp. 39-40, for a description of the *Normandie* fire.

12. Michael Gannon's *Operation Drumbeat* tells the wolf-pack story.

Landmarking

The final battles of World War II were still to be fought when plans were announced in December 1944 to replace the so-called Rhinelander Row of five Greek Revival townhouses on Washington Square North with a 28-story apartment building. MacDougal Alley would be obliterated in the process. The public hulla-baloo that erupted eventually resulted in a compromise, thanks in part to Robert Moses in his dual role as commissioner of parks and city planning. His proposed zoning amendment limited the height of buildings facing parks so there would be no more "Chinese walls around New York's little open spaces."[1] The new, less-intrusive plan was engineered by architects Harvey Wiley Corbett and Robert Weinstein, owner of number 21 just three houses from the demolition site. (Twenty-one years earlier, Corbett had preserved the visual scale and rhythm of the block east of Fifth Avenue. He did this by saving the Greek Revival facades of the houses in The Row that he converted into an apartment building for the trustees of Sailors' Snug Harbor.) A five-story, red-brick, Greek Revival–inspired structure took the place of the century-old houses that had faced Washington Square. Around the corner, a garden and three additional classic homes including the one built by John Taylor Johnston—the city's first marble-clad residence—were torn down to make way for the 20-story, gray-brick building at 2 Fifth Avenue. MacDougal Alley survived and, viewed from the park, the five-story wing appears to reduce the mass of the tower that was completed in 1952.

Robert Moses's 1951 plan to clean up what he considered slums in the south Village would have leveled nearly all of the 40 or so acres between West Fourth and Spring Streets, Sixth Avenue, and Mercer Street. MacDougal and Sullivan Streets would have disappeared, while a widened West Broadway, linked to Fifth Avenue via a roadway cut through Washington Square, would have carried two-way automobile and bus traffic. The resulting uproar, led by another team of prominent architects who lived in the Village, put the kibosh on all but one giant corner of this scheme to create a huge high-rise residential district inaptly named Washington Square Village. A walk along Bleecker Street between Mercer and LaGuardia Place (as this segment of West Broadway is known today) shows what the commissioner may have had in mind—block after block of massive, institutional-style apartment complexes that tower over the surrounding neighborhood.

If Moses had had his way, as he almost always did, the four-lane highway through the park would have resulted in a change of name for West Broadway to Lower Fifth Avenue, a far more attractive address for real estate developers. Villagers, infuriated by this latest show of Moses's audacity, banded together in the many-pronged Joint Emergency Committee that succeeded by November 1958 in closing the park to vehicular traffic, except bicycles, for the first time since 1870.[2]

Victory for the Ladies in Tennis Shoes

Preservationists were shocked in 1950 when the city's best-loved hotel, Warren and Wetmore's Ritz Carlton, was replaced on Madison and Forty-Sixth Street by an office building. In 1954, Richard Morris Hunt's Tenth Street Studios, clubhouse for five generations of American artists, was demolished for a commonplace apartment house. Soon to fall was James Renwick's charming Rhinelander Gardens, a row of eight three-story houses unified by two tiers of intricate cast-iron balconies and set back from West Eleventh Street by deep gardens.

The destruction of Pennsylvania Station, over a two-year period beginning in 1963, aroused many previously indifferent Manhattanites to the steady loss of their architectural heritage. The station, as Robert Hughes wrote in *American Visions*, was the grandest design by far of the distinguished firm of McKim, Mead, & White. Its waiting room was an enlarged replica of the Baths of Caracalla in Rome; the soaring vaults of glass and iron that covered the passenger concourse "were a crystalline

*Pennsylvania Station,
McKim, Mead & White's
grandest design, was
demolished in the 1960s
in a "monumental act of
vandalism."*

spectacle that surpassed anything else of the kind built in America."

"Until the first blow fell," a *New York Times* editorial said on October 30, 1963, "no one was convinced that Penn Station really would be demolished or that New York would permit this monumental act of vandalism. . . . We will probably be judged not by the monuments we build but by those we have destroyed." In a letter to the Times, the president of the financially beleaguered Pennsylvania Railroad asked, "Does it make any sense to preserve a building merely as a 'monument'?" However insensitive that railroad executive might sound today, in mid-century he was championing progress and "the American way." Harmon Goldstone, who would become the second chairman of the Landmarks Preservation Commission, said that at the time "only a handful, a tiny handful, of people" were interested in the history of New York. "The prevailing image of preservationists," he added, "was of ladies with tennis shoes and floppy hats, joined by a few crackpots."[3]

Preservation, what there was of it, usually meant the restoration of a historic prize such as Fraunces Tavern by the Sons of the Revolution or Dyckman House, the last Dutch farmhouse in Manhattan, by the Dyckman family. As Gregory F. Gilmartin notes in his *Shaping the City*, preservation meant "condemning historic buildings to the eerie half-life of a house museum."

Architect Giorgio Cavaglieri, who transformed the glorious but abandoned Jefferson Market Courthouse on Sixth Avenue at Tenth Street into a branch of the city library system in the 1960s, had a different slant on restoration. "Why preserve it," he asked, "if it has no use?"[4] Finding an alternative life for a landmark was a new idea.

Preservationists had begun to win little-noticed but significant victories in the middle 1950s. The U.S. Supreme Court, acting against a local businessman who challenged a slum clearance project in Washington, D.C., ruled, "It is well within the power of the legislature to determine that the community should be beautiful as well as healthy." In 1956, the New York State Legislature approved the Bard Law, named for Alfred Bard, a voice braving the wilderness of preservation since the 1890s. It allowed municipalities to enact "special regulations for the protection, enhancement, perpetuation" of buildings having historic or aesthetic value.

When the city planning commission was set to replace the outmoded 1916 zoning law in the late 1950s, Greenwich Village and Brooklyn Heights campaigned for inclusion of historic zones. "Politically impossible," warned Commissioner James Felt. But he promised to do something about preservation once the new zoning law was in place. Felt kept his word, prevailing upon Mayor Robert Wagner to appoint a committee whose work would eventually lead to legislation to create the Landmarks Preservation Commission. A draft of the bill was placed on the mayor's desk in May 1964. Finally, in October, it was delivered to the city council where it was approved unanimously in April 1965 and signed by Mayor Wagner. There never was a chance that the new law would save Penn Station, but had it moved more expeditiously through city hall, the Brokow Mansion might still be standing. One of the last great Fifth Avenue mansions and the cornerstone of a superb blockfront at Seventy-Ninth Street fell to a wrecking crew on a February weekend in 1965.

Under the legal mechanism formulated for the Landmarks Preservation Commission, after public hearings, the commission has the authority to designate buildings of historic significance. Once a building has been designated as a landmark, prior approval of the commission is needed for even minor alterations. The U.S. Supreme Court upheld the constitutionality of the preservation law in a 1978 ruling about Grand Central Terminal. The terminal owner, the Penn Central Railroad, filed suit when the commission rejected its proposal to build a 54-story tower over the rotunda and concourse.

By September 1965, the new commission was cautiously preparing to test its powers. The U.S. Steel Corporation had recently bought the slender and striking 47-story Singer Tower, built in 1908 at Broadway and Liberty Street by the sewing machine company.[5] Rumor had it that U.S. Steel planned to demolish the tower for something modern. The commission ignored the rumors about Singer, but not those about Sailors' Snug Harbor, whose trustees were said to be planning to tear down the row of five Greek Revival dormitories on Staten Island.[6] On September 21, the commission held public hearings on its plan to designate the dormitories and the nearby chapel as landmarks, despite strenuous objections by the trustees.

Harbor trustees were not the only ones on the commission's carpet at that initial hearing. The Friends Meeting House on Gramercy Park was to be sold by its Quaker owners to a developer as was the Astor Library, bought in the 1920s by the Hebrew Immigrant Aid Society. The Lutheran Church, which had inherited the J. P. Morgan mansion on Madison at Thirty-Seventh Street, planned to demolish the historic structure. The Manhattan Club wanted to sell its home, the former Jerome mansion on Madison Square. Only the Manhattan Club, which was able to prove hardship in court, came down when the commission was unable to find a buyer for it. The other buildings survived because of the landmarks law.

The president of the Harbor trustees, Walter P. Pease—a Manhattan lawyer and also president of the chamber of commerce—declared that the row of dormitories "is not a museum and does not have any historical significance." Captain James Hanna of The Marine Society was the only trustee to argue that the architectural value of the buildings was such that at least their facades should be saved. The board offered a compromise. Minard Lafever's original building would be retained as administrative headquarters along with the chapel.[7]

On October 14, at the commission's first designation hearing, the six Staten Island buildings were designated as landmarks—an action that started a series of lawsuits and complicated negotiations between the city and the Harbor that lasted nearly six years. (In 1973, the Victorian gatehouse and the seven-foot fence that encloses 20 acres of Harbor land were designated by the city as landmarks. The gatehouse was built in 1874, and the fence dates to 1842.)

Troubles in the Postwar Years

The physical properties of Sailors' Snug Harbor, both on Manhattan and on Staten Island, had deteriorated sadly during the years of deferred maintenance ordained by depression and war. In addition, the board of trustees itself was not in good condition. Its two clerical members were old and ailing. The president, a businessman who, by tradition, headed both the chamber of commerce and the board of trustees, was about to complete his dual two-year terms. Mayor William O'Dwyer, like most of his twentieth-century predecessors, never attended meetings. The state office of chancellor and the city office of recorder had been abolished years ago. So, in large part, two retired sea captains were responsible for the institution's affairs. The Harbor began to depend, more than ever before, on the advice of consultants.

Early in 1946, the trustees began discussing a plan to charge Harbor residents as a way of meeting increasing operational costs. In his farewell to the board, President Leroy A. Lincoln questioned a policy that would have "this great institution with its very substantial endowments, resort to such means to acquire what would be a relatively small enhancement of its funds." But the board had hired a team of consulting social workers and it went along with the recommendation that those who could pay should pay. For the first time in Harbor history, not all the old mariners were penniless. Some received Social Security payments and even small pensions. They would now be required to sign a "property agreement," in which their savings and pensions would be surrendered in return for room and board and a monthly allowance of $15. Applicants with independent means of $2,000 or more were required to include the Harbor in their wills. Residents who refused to sign the property agreement could be expelled. Even though the plan had been approved by the state attorney general, it was ill conceived. The maritime unions, at the urging of Harbor residents, convinced the attorney general that it would be good policy to reverse his approval of the plan. He did, and brought suit in state supreme court charging that the Harbor's financial problems were due to mismanagement and waste. The trustees agreed to withdraw the plan to charge residents. (In 1967, the court empowered the trustees to charge residents who "are financially able to contribute" with these limitations: payments need not be made out of the principal of any savings or assets; mariners shall retain a reasonable amount of personal funds for living expenses not covered by the Harbor. In addition, the judgment allowed wives to live with their husbands in the Harbor.)

The *New York Times* Scoops the Harbor

Consultants cannot be blamed for the board's next public embarrassment, one reported by Richard H. Parke in the *New York Times* on January 14, 1949. He wrote: "A 27-year-old Presbyterian minister has been trying unsuccessfully for more than a year to compel Sailors' Snug Harbor to admit him to its board of trustees in accordance with its charter. The minister is the Rev. John O. Mellin . . . pastor of the First Presbyterian Church." The article reported that both Mellin and the Reverend Theodore F. Savage, Stated Clerk of the Presbytery, had informed the Harbor that on the death of the Reverend Julius Moldenhawer in 1948 Mellin had become pastor of First Presbyterian and, as such, would succeed Moldenhawer on the board of trustees. Mellin never got an answer to his letter and Savage received a one-sentence acknowledgment. In a follow-up article the next day, the Times reported that Harbor comptroller Theodore Sicama and a lawyer had visited Mellin late in the afternoon of the day the story broke to explain that there had been a "misunderstanding of terms." Mellin attended his first board meeting on January 22, 1949.

In an interview in 1996 at his retirement home on Cape Cod, Mellin, looking more like a good-natured lumberjack than a second-generation clergyman, recalled how the Times got its story. Rents on some Harbor properties in Greenwich Village increased at the beginning of the year, including the apartment where reporter Richard H. Parke lived. Parke wanted an explanation and Mellin lived nearby, so he called him and unearthed a bit of hanky panky. Mellin said that for months the board had been run as a private fief by the Reverend Frederic S. Fleming of Trinity Church, "an old curmudgeon," and the sea captains "who sat around drinking coffee and collecting fees for attending unnecessary weekly meetings." Meanwhile, President James G. Blaine had been in Europe for nearly a year on an assignment for the Economic Cooperation Administration.

The Reverend John Mellin got his trusteeship through The New York Times.

Mellin's problems obtaining recognition seem to have been based on two factors. First, the board had hoped for a more seasoned and prominent clergyman. Perhaps more important, Mellin was an activist. He had been among a clergy protest group that tried to stop the destruction of houses on the south side of Washington Square to make way for New York University's (NYU's) law school—this at the very time that the trustees and NYU were discussing long-term leases on Washington Square North.

Downsizing

In 1950, on the advice of architect Harvey Wiley Corbett and hospital consultant Otis N. Auer, 23 of the 70 buildings on the old Staten Island farmland were bulldozed as part of a "modernization and improvement plan."

The Harbor had been rigorously self-sufficient from its beginning, but the end of that institutional style was signaled on May 10, 1950, when 42 Holsteins, 36 pigs, and an unknown number of chickens were sold and delivered to nearby farmers. Stables, barns, silos, and many outbuildings were torn down as was the blacksmith's shop and the powerhouse that had supplied electricity. From here on, power would be purchased from the city. Termites had undermined the mansions of the governor and the physician, so both were leveled. Because the Harbor population had dropped well below 300, the large and obsolescent hospital-sanitarium complex was demolished, to be replaced by a smaller, modern facility.

Staten Islanders had watched the diminution of the Harbor estate in silent amazement until learning that the demolition list included Randall Memorial Church ("the Memorial"), for them a beloved landmark whose dome floated above the island's treetops. The Memorial, built in 1890 at a cost of $225,000 and insured, with contents, for $489,600, had long been a financial burden on the trustees. As the minutes of a board meeting reported in 1947, "Its size and cost of maintenance are greatly out of proportion to the number of mariners attending services—The chapel is more in accordance with our needs." Led by the borough president, Staten Islanders came up with a number of "save the Memorial" proposals. All were either unfeasible or underfunded.

Overhauling Management

Basic administrative reorganizations were carried out in the mid-1950s—first, on the advice of Community Research Associates and, then, by McKinsey & Company. An experienced social service executive was appointed deputy to the sea-captain governor in 1953. An occupational therapist and a social director were added to the staff. The newly created position of executive manager took over the traditional trustee chore of dealing with individual leases.

In 1958, McKinsey conducted a thorough and troublesome shakeup. No longer would the governor be chief of administration on Staten Island. That responsibility shifted to the newly created director's office. As chief executive officer, as well as secretary and treasurer, the director would be in charge of the affairs and property of the corporation and of all officers other than the board president. The governor became an assistant director, as did the head of the real estate operation in Manhattan. Theodore Sicama, long the comptroller and more recently the new executive manager, was elected director.

Within a matter of months, Captain William C. Twigg, the governor since 1955, was told that he would not be reappointed and Sicama was replaced, on McKinsey's recommendation, by Floyd D. Parish, assistant administrator of Meriden Hospital in Connecticut. Parish lasted seven months. It may not have been coincidental that his fall followed a written report about Harbor operations by the firm of Randall & Daniels, a social services placement group in New York. Frederick I. Daniels took over Parish's post on a consulting basis while maintaining his connection with the placement firm.

Frequent executive turnover had been unheard of in the Harbor's ear-

A Harbor "downsizing" included demolition of the Randall Memorial Church.

A "snug" views the ruins of Randall Memorial Church.

lier years. Between 1837 and 1948, the top management office of comptroller had been filled by only four occupants: Joseph Greenleaf
(1837-71), his son Thomas Greenleaf (1872-1903), James Henry
(1903-22), and Walter Guenther (1922-48). Guenther was succeeded by
his assistant, Theodore Sicama. Albert E. Buck, the real estate manager, took
early retirement in 1960 after 42 years of service.

Troubled Neighbors and Lawsuits

In 1961, neighboring resident associations from Randall Manor and
the Livingston Community urged the trustees to support a zoning
change that would limit to garden apartments construction within 600
feet of the Harbor's western boundary and 500 feet of its southern border. The trustees were not interested. They already had a plan to turn
that unused 15-acre tract on the Harbor's southwest corner into an
income producer. A letter of agreement had been signed with a developer who would erect a tall luxury apartment building and stores on the
land. Although the deal fell through when rising interest rates made it
difficult to raise money, the neighbors' outcry against the project had
caught the attention of city hall, where it was proposed that the land be
taxed at $100,000 annually if it was not needed for charitable purposes.
By landscaping the property and turning it into a park used by the
mariners, the trustees hoped to escape from the tax rolls. It was not that

simple. Taxes had to be paid for several years before a settlement was reached. Once again, the trustees had incurred an expense where they had expected a profit and they had churned up public and political displeasure.

State law gave the attorney general's office the right to supervise charitable trusts, and in the 1950s it began to carry out this responsibility with a legal vigor that tested the trust's defensive mettle. New York Attorney General Louis Lefkowitz, prompted by the abortive plan to charge the retired seamen for room and board, brought a "mismanagement and waste" suit in the state supreme court against the trustees in 1968. He claimed to have letters and documents from a large number of mariners to support his charges. In an attempt to bolster his suit, he listened to Admiral Edward Holden, once a trustee and now a tenant of the Harbor made bitter by hard times. Holden called to Lefkowitz's attention a 1963 management survey by Executive Assets, Inc., that he said had been ignored by the board. In truth, the survey had been discussed at length before being shelved "as naive and of poor quality." Lefkowitz's failure to produce any of the documents he had cited led to a dismissal. When Lefkowitz appealed to the appellate division, the trustees invited the attorney general's office to inspect their books and records with the help of the Harbor's auditors. After an entire summer examining the books, Lefkowitz conceded that nothing had been found to support his charges. Again, the case was dismissed.

On another legal front, the trustees were victorious in their challenge to the Landmarks Preservation Commission's designation of the six Staten Island buildings. The state supreme court ruled in May 1967 that "the cost of preservation cannot be thrust upon the land owner." An appeal by the city on the commission's behalf was supported by the Municipal Art Society. The issue was brought to an impasse 10 months later when Justice Aaron Steuer, writing for the appellate division, called for additional testimony. A new round of discovery was ordered to determine whether landmarking "either physically or financially prevents or seriously interferes with carrying out [its] charitable purpose."

One paragraph in Steuer's opinion delighted preservationists. It reads: "We deem certain of the basic questions raised to be no longer arguable. In this category is the right, within proper limitations, of the state to place restrictions on the use being made by an owner of his property for the cultural and esthetic benefit of the community." As Frank Gilbert, then commission secretary, recalled recently, "This was

Magna Carta for us at a time when everything about landmarking was up in the air."

As for the Harbor, all the legal, cultural, and political commotion had divided the loyalties of residents, creating frustration for themselves, the staff, and the administrators. Harbor Governor Sidney Trew resigned in June 1969. The board had decided earlier that the next governor or assistant director would be a specialist in gerontology. The Reverend John Mellin, by now a trustee with 22 years' seniority, was in full agreement until, as he explained in the Cape Cod interview, "A sharp young captain from the Marine Society took me to lunch at India House and convinced me that we should consider Leo Kraszeski, the Society's second vice president, for the governorship." Captain Kraszeski took office on July 1, 1969. He rescued an institution that was precariously adrift.

Notes

1. Robert A. M. Stern, *New York 1960*, p. 221.

2. See Emily Kies Folpe, *It Happened on Washington Square.*

3. An interview with Anthony C. Wood, board member of the Preservation League of New York State and of the Greenwich Village Society for Historic Preservation; Gregory F. Gilmartin, *Shaping the City: A History of the Municipal Art Society*; and Barbarlee Diamonstein, *Landmarks of New York* provided the grounding for the landmarks section.

4. Cavaglieri's comment was made at a celebration of the Jefferson Market Library on its thirtieth anniversary on February 25, 1998.

5. Elliot Willensky and Norval White's *AIA Guide to New York City* called the demolition of the Singer Tower the "city's greatest loss since Penn Station."

6. The public learned about the demolition plans in July 1950 when the *Staten Island Advance* ran the first of many articles on the "modernization" plan. The report on the sale of the farm animals in May was a tip-off on what was to come.

7. In the late 1980s, Captain Leo Kraszeski wrote a 14-page "historical overview" about decisions made by the board of trustees beginning in the 1930s. These pages are based on that overview, trustee minutes, and *Staten Island Advance* articles.

THE VOYAGE TO SEA LEVEL

Seven years before Captain Leo Kraszeski assumed the governorship of Sailors' Snug Harbor in 1969, he had turned down the job. In the intervening years, as second vice president of The Marine Society, he was in a special position to observe developments that brought the Harbor to its historic low ebb.[1]

Aside from the landmark issue and the court cases, congressional enactment of Medicare in 1965 caused costs and standards of institutional care and housing for the elderly to rise significantly. Worse yet, inflation generated by the Vietnam War had a crippling impact on the consolidated 99-year leases that the Harbor had granted to developers in the 1950s and 1960s (199-year leases in two cases). The leases generated fixed annual incomes of 5 percent, a common rate dating to the years following the Civil War. What seemed to be sound business had locked in Harbor income at approximately $1 million a year, earnings no longer sufficient to maintain the old sailors' home where expenses had risen to more than $1.3 million annually. The deficit operation was to last for years.

Captain Leo Kraszeski, the governor who transformed the Harbor, 1969-87.

At the time Kraszeski rejected the governorship in 1962, he was a salvage investigator for a company that insured steamship hulls and cargoes sailing from the port of New York. He found the work to be enjoyable and gratifying and did not feel any need to make a change. He was an active member of the Society of Naval Architects and Engineers. Kraszeski was a 1944 graduate of the U.S. Merchant Marine Academy at Kings Point, and his first voyage as a third mate was on the dangerous run to the Russian port of Murmansk. Later in the Pacific, his ship was torpedoed. By 1946, he had earned his master's license.

When he and his wife Patricia and their eight children moved from Stamford, Connecticut, to Staten Island in the summer of 1969, Kraszeski told the *Staten Island Advance* that it was time to bring some young blood into the Harbor. It soon became evident that the captain had a lot more in mind than finding a pleasant place to raise his children.

The official title of the Harbor governor at the time was assistant director-superintendent, only the fourth-ranking official on the administrative staff and one who did not attend board of trustee meetings except by invitation. Frederick Daniels was still the part-time consulting executive director; Frank L. Hickcock, a veteran of the Harbor's real estate group, was the full-time director; and Ernest Mount, hired a year earlier, was assistant director for real estate and future planning. By mid-September all three had resigned, and Kraszeski had been promoted to acting director. He was elected director two months later.

How did this happen? There was no official explanation, but Kraszeski—a shrewd, confident New Englander—arrived at the Harbor with a set of priorities that the trustees latched onto quickly. The first priority was to reduce expenses by cutting the management deadwood created by consolidation of 225 Manhattan building lots into 18 leases. Second, Harbor officials would begin the difficult job of restoring the physical plant on Staten Island to a workable, cost-effective entity. Third, they would build credibility with the residents. In later years, the captain commented that the officials who resigned had already despaired of the Harbor's future and went looking for something better to do "when this guy with a big mouth came along."

In another phase of the battle against deadwood, Board President Charles Renchard and Kraszeski discussed problems caused by the attendance at monthly meetings of an attorney from the trustees' law firm and the consultant-of-the-day, each charging by the hour. Too often, when a course of action was almost in hand, one or another of the trustees would call for a legal or expert opinion that, invariably, could not be delivered until the next meeting. By that time, the issue had resolved itself, had gotten worse, or no longer mattered. The trustees unanimously adopted a motion to make the meetings more productive and less costly by banning counsel and advisors.

Some months before Kraszeski arrived at the Harbor, Harbor officials had threatened to take legal action against mariners who failed to pay the maintenance charges approved by the state supreme court in 1967. One of Kraszeski's first moves was to urge the board to defer the collection suits while he attempted to persuade the recalcitrant residents about the reasonableness of the fees.

A key element in Kraszeski's long-term strategy began to emerge in 1970—-move the chamber of commerce trustee out of the president's chair. For decades, the new chamber president, elected for two years and nearly always the retiring chairman of a major bank, did double duty by also serving as president of the Harbor board. Even conscientious incumbents had only a brief

Captain Wilbur Dow, Kraszeski's partner and the most influential trustee president since DeWitt Clinton.

time to learn the intricacies of the job. In what was to be a successful, two-pronged maneuver, Renchard, chairman of Chemical Bank and Trust, agreed that if the board was to maintain continuity of thought and direction the president would have to serve more than two years. Next, The Marine Society changed its bylaws to allow officers to serve six instead of three years and it elected Wilbur E. Dow Jr. first vice president, a position that automatically made him a Harbor trustee. Within weeks, Dow succeeded Renchard as president of the board.

Not since the days of DeWitt Clinton had a president come to the Harbor with a background as rich and varied as Dow's. Born in Brooklyn and raised in Seattle, he was sailing in the late 1920s in the global trade of the Isthmian Line where he acquired his master's license. At New York University Law School, he earned a degree as an admiralty lawyer in 1934. Dow argued and won three cases before the U.S. Supreme Court; represented Lloyd's of London in New York for two decades; and, in the years immediately following World War II, bought hundreds of vessels for Aristotle Onassis and other Greek shipowners. He owned and operated excursion lines on Lake George and the Mississippi River and was one of the chief developers of the New Orleans riverfront as a tourist attraction.

Architectural plans to rebuild the Harbor on Staten Island. Only the original Greek Revival building and the chapel would survive.

In 1954, Dow led a trek through Arctic wastes in a sturdy Maine fishing boat to plot precisely the Magnetic North Pole. Previous measurements, made from long distances, showed the Magnetic Pole to be up to 150 miles northwest of the point on Prince of Wales Island where Dow and his seismologist determined it to be. Dow's successor in his later role as the Harbor's general counsel, Dyer S. Wadsworth, was a member of the 11-man "Dow Polar Expedition."[2]

Dow, Kraszeski, and the vice president of the board, John Mellin, were about to embark on a mission to save and transform their troubled institution. Just how troubled the seamen's home had become was demonstrated in 1972 when the Reverend Robert Ray Parks came up from Jacksonville, Florida, to become the fifteenth rector of Trinity Church and thus a Harbor trustee. Parks recalled recently that members of his vestry advised him against becoming actively involved in Harbor affairs. There was talk on Wall Street, he was told, about the mishandling of Harbor funds. Dow and Kraszeski visited the new rector and they talked at length. Parks was much impressed by the two captains and became an active board member. It was his belief that the institution would have gone bankrupt if the trustees had tried to stay in Staten Island.

The Mayor Comes Aboard

Minutes from the January 1962 board meeting carried the following fretful but prophetic passage: "It may be desirable to consider new facilities in a new location because of the obsolescence and inefficiency of the present Harbor buildings, the changing needs of the Mariners, and the changing character of Staten Island. Resolved that a study be made."

The study, and others that followed, led to the hiring in 1964 of the architectural firm of Edward H. Noakes & Associates to develop a plan that would convert the classic structure of the Harbor into a suburban, waterfront community with three ten-story residential buildings plus clusters of residences. Architectural artwork that has survived in the archives shows, along with the residential structures, an infirmary and a community services building, each at four stories. Except for the original 1833 Greek Revival building and the chapel, demolition was to be the fate of all other buildings on the grounds, including the four newer members of the famed Greek Revival row. This was the plan that caught the attention of the newly empowered Landmarks Preservation Commission.

New York Mayor John Lindsay came up with a plan to change the old sailors' home into a city-owned cultural center.

The commission's decision to save the historic buildings put Noakes's plan on hold. Within days of the state supreme court's ruling in May 1967 against designating the Harbor buildings as landmarks, the trustees instructed the architect to continue with his plans. Noakes was still at his drawing board in March 1968 when the court of appeals called for further testimony on the landmarking question.

At this point, Mayor John V. Lindsay stepped into the dispute with a plan of his own. In November 1968, the mayor, his corporation counsel, and the two top officials of the Landmarks Preservation Commission attended a meeting of the Harbor board of trustees. Geoffrey Platt, the commission's chairman, conceded that the four Greek Revival dormitories flanking the original building could not be altered successfully for use by the Harbor. The minutes are not clear about what happened next, but it seems that someone suggested that the trust donate all five buildings and about nine acres of land to the city for a proposed cultural center. Lindsay emphasized that the Harbor would be relieved of any obligation to maintain the buildings if they became city property. Creating the center would require an estimated $4 million, he said, most of which would come from a fund-raising drive and part from the capital budget of the Staten Island Institute of Arts and Sciences and its museum.

Obviously, the suggestion about donating Harbor property was not taken seriously by either side. On February 1, 1971, Lindsay announced that the city was about to begin negotiations with the trustees to buy the six land-marked buildings plus the auditorium, the recreation hall, and more than 13 acres of land for a cultural center. The amount of land was extended to 15 acres after Harbor negotiators pointed out that the city plan over-looked one vital piece of property—the powerhouse that supplied the other buildings with heat and water.

Shortly after moving into city hall in January 1966, Lindsay formally announced his refusal to serve as a trustee. Two years later, he changed his mind. The mayor said his duties still made it impossible for him to attend meetings but a nonvoting representative, Holt Meyer, director of Staten Island development, would represent him when the board con-vened.

The Choice: Scylla or Charybdis

The final phase of the Harbor's long residency on Staten Island was kicked off early in 1970 by a letter from the New York State Department of Health instructing the trustees to build a new infirmary to replace the existing nonfunctional firetrap. The board was caught in the middle. It could not afford to build a modern 120-bed facility unless heavy main-tenance expenses were reduced by tearing down the Greek temples, a move that the Landmarks Preservation Commission would not allow.

In a letter published in the *Staten Island Advance* on July 8, 1970, Wilbur Dow wrote:"We do not want a fancy new building to replace our current structures but something safe and in accordance with modern nursing standards and present requirements of aged people. . . .The clas-sic Greek Revival buildings are nothing more than Hollywood false fronts preventing the public from seeing the miserable conditions behind them."

To dramatize the problem caused by the conflicting views of the health department and the landmarks commission, Noakes was called upon to design an infirmary and a home within the old buildings. Interiors would be stripped and rebuilt, an additional floor added to the one-story hyphens or connecting passageways, and windows great-ly enlarged. The health department, which would have had to reim-burse part of the expense, found the renovation plan far too costly. Not surprisingly, the Landmarks Preservation Commission would have none of it.

Kraszeski and the board never really expected the plan to be accepted. Many years later, Kraszeski explained that the rebuilding plan was a "tongue-in-cheek effort to precipitate something." That it did. Having demonstrated the unlikelihood of ever satisfying both state and city agencies, the board could claim that it now had little choice but to leave Staten Island. In October, the trustees instructed Dow and Kraszeski to seek out a new location. After a brief look at a closed seminary on the Hudson above Poughkeepsie, New York, they decided to find a site on the Atlantic coast somewhere between Charleston, South Carolina, and Norfolk, Virginia. Florida was too hot, and any place north of Norfolk was too industrial and had a climate no better than that of Staten Island.

The Search Begins

Letters seeking a 10-acre site for a home and infirmary went to the appropriate chambers of commerce. Several sites looked promising, with Charleston first on the inspection list. Whatever chance this bastion of southern gentility had of becoming the new location for the Sailors' Snug Harbor was badly hurt by a nursing-home strike that began the very day Dow and Kraszeski arrived to survey the health-care scene. In reality, neither Charleston nor any of the other sites put forward by their chambers of commerce had a chance of beating the eventual winner, a North Carolina backwater called Sea Level.

Just before Dow was to meet Kraszeski in Charleston, he went to Florida on business. While there he visited a one-time legal client, Dan Taylor, head of a family conglomerate that owned a Caribbean shipping line, plus interests in railroad lines, hotels, race horses, and a company that supplied salt to northern highway departments. A Sea Level native, Taylor had built and operated the first community hospital and the first motel in the area, and he was the visionary behind a plan to turn it into a retirement center. As a board member of the Pennsylvania Railroad, which owned property in the neighborhood, Taylor was attempting to persuade his peers to invest in a community of small homes and apartments for retired railroad workers. The keystone of his plan was to turn his 80-bed country hospital into a general teaching center with acute-care, surgery, and emergency-room services. This he accomplished by donating the hospital he had built five years earlier plus 1,500 acres of land to the Duke University Medical Center 200 miles away in Durham. Duke, which had recently received a Ford Foundation grant to pursue

community-health activities, was pleased to sign a 20-year agreement
with Taylor. Duke's Sea Level operation was just getting under way when
Dow and Kraszeski accepted Taylor's invitation to visit.

What they found was a land of tall pines on Nelson's Bay, 20 minutes by ferry to the Outer Banks and 20 miles to the handsome little
port city of Beaufort, the nearest shopping and entertainment center,
and an offer they could not refuse. For $50,000, Taylor would provide 35
usable acres for a modern home and nursing facility plus 70 acres of
scenic marsh. Once the Harbor was in operation, he would return the
$50,000 payment. That offer, plus an affiliation with Duke, just up the
road, sealed the deal. Duke's commitment was to make its hospital and
medical staff available to the Harbor. On its own merits, the Harbor's
nursing home was good; with Duke it could be great.

At its November 1970 meeting, Dow told the board that building in
Sea Level would be much cheaper than on Staten Island, and the annual cost of maintaining the residents—about $9,000 each—would be cut
in half. The board unanimously accepted Taylor's offer. In March 1971, its
new law firm—Dewey, Ballantine, Busby, Palmer and Wood—petitioned
the surrogate court for permission to relocate to North Carolina. Dow
hoped to see a decision in a matter of weeks. Because of stubborn opposition by Attorney General Louis Lefkowitz, more than a year and a half
passed before the move was approved. Lefkowitz argued against the
"remoteness" of the hamlet of Sea Level. His assistant in charge of charitable foundations, Warren M. Goidel, charged that the only beneficiaries
of the shift southward would be developers in North Carolina.
Counterargument came from the president of Duke University and,
somewhat unexpectedly, from the New York State Department of
Health. Both testified in favor of the move to a site next door to Duke's
Sea Level Hospital. That very point was the chief one cited by Surrogate
S. Samuel DiFalco in his decision favoring the move. The case for relocation was "overwhelming," he said.

Challenging Randall's Will

During the long debate about where the old sailors should live, two
other petitions were filed with the courts seeking permission to sell
Harbor property on Staten Island as well as the supposedly sacrosanct
land in Manhattan. No one before had ever challenged the belief that
Captain Randall's will forbade forever the sale of his 21-acre Manhattan
farm. DiFalco, citing the *cy pres* legal doctrine, found that because

circumstances had changed since the will was written he had the power to direct a disposition that "will most effectively accomplish the testator's charitable intent." Support for the old sailors' asylum would soon depend upon the sale of the Manhattan leaseholds. Proceeds would be held in perpetuity by the Randall Endowment trust fund.

The Staten Island property, appraised at $7.6 million, was first on the market. Sigmund Sommer, a developer who had built skyscrapers in Manhattan and private homes in New Jersey, contracted in spring 1972 to pay the Harbor $6.2 million for 65 of the 80 acres. The city took over the remaining 15 acres and the buildings on them for $1.8 million. As part of the deal, the board agreed to give up its court fight to overturn the landmark designation in exchange for a waiver from the city for back taxes on the southwest corner of the Staten Island property.

Number One Fifth Avenue towers over Washington Square and Giuseppe Garabaldi, a gift of the Italian community.

Sommer's plan to build a series of six-story apartments with 2,800 luxury units angered and frightened nearby residents. They organized and protested loudly to the mayor and borough officials about the intrusion of apartment buildings into a neighborhood of single-family homes. Inspirational support came from artist and photographer John Noble, who anchored his houseboat studio off the Staten Island shore. He had sailed on some of the last schooners to work the Atlantic coast, and many of his old shipmates had retired to the Harbor. An impassioned essay by Noble on the need to save the grounds from development circulated widely and bolstered the argument that all 80 acres should be reserved for a park and cultural center. In June 1973, six months after the mayor turned down a request by the Staten Island Improvement Board to buy Sommer's holdings, he reversed himself and announced a plan to turn the 80 acres into a national showplace of culture and education. The total price of the land was $9.7 million, nearly $2 million more than it would have cost had the purchase been made when the property was first offered.

What changed the perspective of the man who said in January, "For the City to undertake acquisition and maintenance of the remaining 65 acres of this site is beyond our means at this time, given the desperate need for other essential projects"? Following his failed bid for the Democratic presidential nomination in 1972, Lindsay had decided to retire politically and resume his law practice. But he wanted to leave behind some kind of monument to his 15 years of public service as congressman from Manhattan's east side and mayor. How he came to focus on Snug Harbor was outlined in an interview with Terence H. Benbow, dean emeritus of the Quinnipiac School of Law in Connecticut, who, in 1973, was president of Staten Island's Institute of Arts and Sciences and chairman of the New York Landmarks Conservancy.

Benbow; Judge Holt Meyer, then Lindsay's man on Staten Island; Corporation Counsel J. Lee Rankin; landmarks commissioner Harmon Goldstone; and others in the administration and on the island convinced the mayor that the Greek Revival buildings were a citywide, indeed a national, asset that just happened to sit on the north shore of Richmond County. They argued that not only would preservation be worthwhile and notable, but the city would be rid of the Harbor trustees' nagging lawsuit against city landmarking. Once Lindsay took that first 15-acre bite, Benbow said, "It was almost inevitable that he would see the absolute logic and common sense in the fact that you would need the whole 80 acres if you're to have something of national significance."

Not everyone saw it Benbow's way. He recalls that the Staten Island borough president, Robert T. Connor, was more upset about the mayor "intruding" in his backyard than he was about the possible bulldozing of the Harbor's classic row. Holt Meyer remembers that when Lindsay decided to buy all 80 acres, his budget director, David Grossman, walked out of the meeting complaining, "This is much too much culture for Staten Island."

The Manhattan land, encumbered by leases, had been appraised at $13 million. Harbor trustees declined a bid of $17 million from Harry Helmsley's real estate empire for the entire leasehold. The trustees' strategy called for each lease to be sold individually, usually to the leaseholders, a tactic that was to pay off handsomely. On July 7, 1976, the leased land under 1 Fifth Avenue was sold for $1,275,000, well above its appraised value. That was the first sale. When the last parcel was sold in July in 1986, the total value of the old farm—no longer encumbered by leases—had reached $27 million. Minus expenses, the sum of $24,520,530.60 became the Randall Endowment. Not bad for a board that had often been accused of mismanagement.

In another display of financial serendipity, the trust profited admirably by investing profits from its Staten Island properties in discounted short-term bonds dumped on an inflated market at prices well below face value. At maturity, the full-face payoffs generated so much cash-in-hand that the trust began to act as a mortgage broker for some purchasers of its Manhattan leases.

In one instance an investor put $200,000 down on the $750,000 price of two Broadway properties, then was unable to secure a mortgage on reasonable terms for the remaining money. The trust provided him with a 10-year mortgage that would eventually earn $1.3 million in principal and interest payments. The tenants' association of the cooperative apartment house named for A.T. Stewart was granted a $2 million, 10-year, 8 percent mortgage. Annual income for the Harbor jumped to $160,000 from the $60,000 it had earned on the lease. Later, the Harbor extended the mortgage for another five years at 8.5 percent and made a loan for repairs of $2.5 million at 9 percent to Stewart House. The other leaseholds were sold on similar or better terms.

Action at Sea Level

Work on the Sea Level site was under way even before the go-ahead came from the surrogate court. A general contractor was hired, land cleared, and architectural surveys made. Groundbreaking ceremonies for the new home and infirmary took place on July 4, 1973. A $1.5 million line of credit from the European-American Bank and Trust completed financing for the $6 million project. Even the Internal Revenue Service pitched in with some timely news by granting the trust's appeal to be classified as a charitable foundation. The ruling canceled $200,000 in unpaid taxes, plus penalties, interest, and $40,000 annually in future taxes.

Dan Taylor died in the winter of 1973. While he lived, Dow and Kraszeski gave little thought to the 8,000 acres of Taylor-owned property across the highway from the Harbor's building site. Now it became a worry. What might have been part of a railroad retirement community was to be sold piecemeal by the surviving Taylors. The remote possibility of a saloon or liquor store being built on one of the lots sparked preventive action from the Harbor. The Harbor offered the Taylors $1 million, about half of what they expected the property to earn over time,

Main gate to the Sea Level grounds and entrance to the modern home for old mariners.

for the entire 8,000 acres plus the Sea Level Motel. Not only did the Taylor family accept the offer, but the brothers agreed to honor, in part, Dan's promise of a $50,000 rebate when the asylum became operational. Eventually the cost of the site would be reduced to $25,000.

Sailors' Snug Harbor and Duke University now owned all the Taylor family's Sea Level property. Dow and two executives from Duke, both physicians, met to discuss possible joint projects. Dow's letter in the board minutes of June 11, 1974, makes good reading.

> We discussed a development along the lines of Hilton Head, South Carolina, [which] is about the same size as our joint properties. It is largely oriented to affluent adults. I suggested that we might consider something more family oriented with small or medium size playgrounds within walking distance of most homes, with one full size golf course and possibly an additional 9 holes. On the same acreage, Hilton Head has three full size courses.
>
> Dr. Sessions suggested that low or wet places on our properties be scooped out, the surrounding land raised with what was taken from the bottom, and the ponds allowed to fill and then be stocked with bass which the state supplies. The mosquitoes then disappear. It occurs to me that this was exactly what I had seen done at Hilton Head with far less desirable land than what we have.

The discussion, which began at 8 A.M., went on through dinner. They talked about laying out a network of roads to attract middle-income residential development, about the possibility of tree farming, and about the university's plan to turn the Sea Level Hospital into a "fat farm" (a term that Dow had never heard before). First, the plan called for building a new and larger medical facility, along with homes for doctors and nurses, on 200 acres directly across the road from the original hospital that would specialize in the treatment of seriously overweight young children.

Shipping Out

Construction problems at Sea Level delayed the scheduled departure of the mariners from Staten Island for seven months. The transfer to modern quarters finally got under way late in June 1976. Offered a choice between bus and plane, 30 old sailors chose the 14-hour scenic route. A physician, a nurse, and three aides accompanied them. The remaining 75 seamen and their medical team flew to North Carolina four days later. A half-dozen Harbor residents opted to remain in the New York area. Two of them, John Bugel and Anthony Pujol, refused for several days to leave the Harbor grounds. They made the front pages when a sympathetic Jacqueline Kennedy Onassis visited them. She had been an influential supporter of the campaign to landmark the Harbor.

A small fleet of moving vans transported the men's personal belongings along with a valuable collection of crated nineteenth-century marine paintings, heavy-glass display cases that held antique ship models and other maritime artifacts (including a siren from the captain's bridge of the World War II German battleship *Graf Spee* and nineteenth-century navigation equipment), plus the billiard tables. Included among the paintings were six by Antonio Jacobsen, a popular and prolific painter of vessels that visited the port of New York between 1873 and 1919, and several by E. F. Neilson. A large stained-glass window inscribed with the Harbor's seal, *Portum Petimus Fessi* ("We who are weary seek a harbor"), also made the trip. Augustus Saint-Gauden's massive bronze statue of Robert Richard Randall would follow at a later date. First a cast was made for the duplicate bronze that now stands on the original marble pedestal at the cultural center. Randall's remains, buried beneath a granite obelisk, were left in place. Most of the furnishings were sold at auction, including a huge mahogany four-poster bed known as "the Melville bed."

*The Sea Level grounds,
with the seamen's home
in the background.*

The Goodhue Children's Center, next-door neighbor to the Harbor, agreed to maintain the cemetery where some 8,000 seamen lie.

The New Home

The board of trustees had instructed Captain Kraszeski to build a "Cadillac." He and his architect, Edward H. Noakes, did just that. Kraszeski was a hands-on overseer, involved every step of the way from planning to completion of the luxurious, single-story brick structure. It consists of four wings running from a central core that has a high-pitched roof. Three of the four wings serve as residences for as many as 120 sailors, a term that includes a few women these days. Each residence wing has four clusters of 10 comfortable, single-person bedrooms with personal heat and air-conditioning controls. Sliding-glass doors form the outer bedroom walls and open onto small patios and gardens. Lounges and recreation areas are part of each cluster. A large central fireplace dominates the main 40-by-50-foot sitting room. Smaller fireplaces are part of the side walls. Adjoining the sitting room is a spacious dining area and a small snack shop known as "The Bumboat." A library opens to a large and gracious lobby and entrance.

The fourth wing contains administrative offices, the infirmary, and a lounge for the 85 staff members. Furnishings are well designed and sturdy. To allow for wheelchairs, there are no steps or tight turning areas. Some residents have automobiles of their own. Others travel to Beaufort and Morehead City in the home's minivans.

The library at Sea Level. The ship model is one of many made by retired seamen at the Harbor.

On a visit to the home, the author met a resident in the parking lot who was putting fishing pole and tackle box into his car. He was heading to a mountain stream, he said, because the fish in the Sea Level waters were not biting.

Sea Level is in the path of the storms that buffet the Cape Hatteras seashore, but the Harbor is as hurricane-proof as a building can be. It was designed to be secure under the worst storm and flooding conditions the area has known. When Hurricane Gloria roared up the coast on September 27, 1985, the local office of emergency management ordered evacuation of the entire county. Sailors' Snug Harbor ignored the order because of the dangers in moving so many aged and sick people. Up the road, Sea Level Hospital moved about 60 patients. Three of the elderly patients died, and others were injured. The Harbor lost trees, but the building and its residents survived without a scratch. In December 1993,

The main lounge with one of the Harbor's many cases displaying nautical artifacts.

a tornado struck, flattening some outbuildings and tearing part of the roof off of the main building. Damage ran to about $1 million.

Management of the new facility was as advanced as the architecture. The advisor in this area was Charles W. Pruitt, who had worked with Dean Robert Ray Parks in Jacksonville, Florida, when St. Paul's Cathedral built a hospital specializing in geriatric research and a housing development for senior citizens. When Parks moved to New York in 1972 to become rector of Trinity Parish, Pruitt came along as deputy administrator for the church and advisor to Sailors' Snug Harbor on real estate and long-term nursing care. At Sea Level, Pruitt helped update century-old ways of caring for the residents. As for the real estate, Pruitt saw Sea Level as a "lovely piece of property" that should be developed with housing attractive to healthy retired couples. Serious consideration was given to the idea, but no action followed. Pruitt was to become the president of the Presbyterian Home and its complex of charities in Oakmont, Pennsylvania. Recently, he recalled that the opening of the home in Sea Level "was appropriate at the time. It worked beautifully for hundreds of thousands of days of care."

Most of the time Sea Level is a tranquil home, surrounded by woodland and azaleas, for about 80 old folks who seem to be content.

Kraszeski had many reasons to be proud of his work, among them that the building was paid for by the day it opened.

A Changing Cast

Wilbur Dow turned 71 in 1977. With the Harbor well settled in its new location, Dow resigned the presidency but he remained general counsel until 1991. The Reverend John Mellin took his place as president.

Mellin and Terry Sanford—former governor of North Carolina, future U.S. senator, and president of Duke University from 1969 to 1985—discussed the relationship of the Harbor and Duke's Sea Level Hospital many times. That relationship turned out to be a disappointment. Duke had counted on earning sizable fees by treating the aging mariners. When residents of the home became seriously ill, however, they were likely to be flown by helicopter to Newport where hospitals were run by the Veterans Administration and the Navy. The long trip, the Harbor had learned, was less expensive than the short one up the road. And, nothing came of the development plans discussed in Dow's letter. In 1990, Duke turned the hospital over to county authorities, who operate it as a long-term nursing home.

No steps or tight turns make for easy wheel-chairing at Sea Level.

Leo Kraszeski would turn 65 in 1987, a coming event that inspired the following resolution by the board of trustees:

> Whereas, in realization that the terms of office are drawing to a close and mindful of the many and valuable services of its Governor and Executive Director, . . . and apprehensive that these services will be unknown . . . to future Trustees, it is felt that they should be briefly set forth here and suitably awarded by those in possession of personal knowledge of those services.
>
> Whereas, . . . Captain Kraszeski's acceptance of the position [when] Harbor finances were in a precarious position after thirteen years of continuous losses in the neighborhood of $300,000 a year and its resources at a point of exhaustion, that the Harbor found itself in eight different law suits, some having continued as long as eleven years, at an annual cost of almost

$90,000, with the physical plant on Staten Island some 120 years of age and extremely vulnerable to fire, with a most onerous labor situation annually made worse by the politically controlled New York City hospitals, all made worse by fast-rising fuel bills, all compelling a move of the facility to a more hospitable and affordable area, and

Whereas, such a move necessitated the selection of the area . . . , the selection of an architect and close consultation in the ultimate design selected, the selection of a contractor and the close supervision of the many subcontractors necessarily engaged in the work followed by the colossal task of moving the entire institution . . . the selection and training of new employees, all this while maintaining careful supervision and much of the responsibility for its financial affairs which included cooperation and advice in connection with the disposal and subsequent reinvestment of the proceeds of some eighteen parcels of New York City real estate, all of which by the present date, have resulted in the financial independence of the Harbor on into the foreseeable future with no present obligation outstanding.

Now Therefore be it resolved that for these services performed, all unforeseen and unforeseeable at the time of his engagement, it is the sense of the present Trustees to reward Captain Kraszeski by a one-time gift of $100,000.

Macramé wall hanging made by a resident of The Harbor.

The captain had been thinking for some time about cutting his workload, but he had no intention of completely turning over his carefully crafted rest home to a stranger. In May 1987, accepting a search committee's recommendation, the trustees elected James L. Watters, a licensed nursing-home administrator, to be the Harbor's executive director as of July 1. At the same time, Kraszeski would take over the newly created watchdog position of secretary-treasurer. According to the trustees' minutes, they recognized the potential for conflict between the new director and his predecessor. The situation, they said, would be closely monitored.

The dock at Sea Level.

As far as Kraszeski was concerned, there was another problem with this new arrangement: he could no longer automatically take part in board discussions. Later in 1987, Captain Frank Shellenbarger, first vice president of The Marine Society, solved the problem. He resigned his vice presidency and Kraszeski, who had been the society's second vice president for years, moved into the vacant slot and the Harbor trusteeship that went with it. Shellenbarger returned to the board in 1992 when he and Kraszeski swapped the two top Marine Society offices. Since then, he has been the president and Kraszeski the first vice president.

The new and the old executive directors did not get along so, after completing a year of service, Watters left and was replaced by another professional nursing home operator, Thomas Katsanis. Although Kraszeski gave up the post of secretary-treasurer when Katsanis signed on, the new executive director had problems with the Harbor staff and resigned in May 1990.

The captain finally found the right person for the job, someone he knew well, F. Patrick Ausband, administrator of Duke's Sea Level Hospital. Rather than move to Durham when Duke closed the operation, he moved down the road and he was still there as the Harbor's executive director at this writing.

After 39 years as a trustee, John Mellin resigned as board member and president at the end of 1988. His service was rewarded with a racy, bright-red convertible that he drove through the streets of Greenwich Village and Cape Cod for years. The new president of the trustees was also the new rector of Trinity Church, the Reverend Daniel Paul Matthews.

Notes

1. Captain Leo Kraszeski's aforementioned "historical overview" and a series of interviews with Captain Kraszeski in Sea Level and at the downtown Millenium (sic) Hilton, his Manhattan headquarters, provided the background for most of this chapter. Details were added by trustee minutes and clippings from the *Staten Island Advance*, and author interviews with Robert Ray Parks, Terence Benbow, Holt Meyer, Charles Pruitt, John Mellin, and Dyer Wadsworth (trustees general counsel).

2. Biographical material for Dow is from The Marine Society files.

New Directions

CHAPTER

10

From very different starting positions, the new president of the board of trustees Daniel Paul Matthews and the new executive director F. Patrick Ausband came to a surprisingly common point of view: Without radical change, the Harbor could no longer fulfill the intent of the will of Robert Richard Randall.

Matthews, a native North Carolinian from the mountain resort area of Asheville, considered Sea Level to be at the end of the world with neither convenience store nor movie theater within walking distance of the old sailors' home. Citing modern gerontological theory, Matthews believed that the best place for a retirement community was in a busy urban center. His favorite example was St. Margaret's House, a high-rise home for the elderly built by Trinity Church on Fulton Street, less than two blocks from New York's South Street Seaport, which he called "a carnival with shops."[1]

The Sea Level home, arguably the finest retirement facility in the United States, had been about three-quarters full in recent years—90 residents for 120 bedrooms. Remoteness may have been part of the problem, but the principal reason for the empty beds was undoubtedly a shift in maritime culture. Unlike the 14,000 seamen cared for in the Harbor over the better part of two centuries, modern sailors with their Social Security checks and pensions were likely to be family men and women with relatives and friends nearby. Even when money was scarce, many old sailors were reluctant to move by themselves to the Harbor.

Leo Kraszeski had sensed the changing environment even before the move from Staten Island. It was not until May 1985, however, that the minutes of a board meeting reflected the new reality: "Discussion: Supplementing the income of eligible seamen needing help but who preferred to continue to live in an area and environment of their choice. Consensus: Such a program was more desirable than expanding the present facility. . . .The Executive Director was instructed to explore the matter."

In January 1992, the trustees decided to develop a supplementary-income plan that eventually would carry the tag "Mariners Outreach Assistance Program." But the project was set aside temporarily when the accounting firm of McGladney & Pullen informed the board that its study of income and expense projections through the year 2000 revealed that the general fund was declining at an alarming rate. Investment income would be inadequate to sustain operations within five or six years, the report concluded. A second study, by Delafield Harvey & Tabell, was even more dismal.

While still at Duke's Sea Level hospital, Ausband was asked to study the Harbor's books and operation. He concluded that, even though investment-portfolio earnings were above expectations, they could no longer keep ahead of health-care inflation. With applications for admission declining, he added, options beyond residential care should be considered. Ausband was offered the executive directorship. He accepted, unlikely as that may seem for someone who knew the problems. But he liked Sea Level. To him it was a fine place to raise a family and an area ripe for development.

The Reverend Daniel Paul Matthews, rector of Trinity Church, succeeded the Reverend John Mellin of First Presbyterian as president of the board of trustees in 1988.

From the beginning of his presidency, Matthews and the board had discussed caring for distressed mariners in ways other than sheltering them in a home for old folks.

The Options

In a perusal of the institutional archives, Kraszeski had come across an article about the Harbor in an 1884 issue of *Century* magazine, the leading literary journal of its day. The author, Franklyn North, who had had a friendly, informative meeting with the governor and many of the mariners, ended his article with a question that was again being asked more than 100 years later by the board of trustees: "Whether the sailor is as happy under the conditions obtaining at a Home as he is with a small pension." The subject had been thrashed out for 160 years by successive boards of the Admiralty of the Royal Navy, North reported, before a decision was made in 1865 to close Greenwich Hospital and use its considerable income to pay hard cash to the superannuated and decrepit seamen that it had sheltered since 1705. "The inauguration of such a stipend system at Sailors' Snug Harbor would, beyond question, give great satisfaction, and many would take advantage of it, live with or near their children or grandchildren in quiet contentment, instead of moping gloomingly about the quadrangle of the Harbor," North concluded.

The time had finally come to give North's suggestion serious consideration. The board instructed Ausband to spell out the choices. The trustees could, he said, continue to operate as usual, gambling that investment income would increase and expenses decline. Alternatively, the home could be closed down over time by admitting no new residents. A strategy for distributing investment income would be developed while waiting for the current sojourners to die. He concluded that the only reasonable option was to institute an assistance program that allowed needy mariners to age in a place of personal choice.[2]

F. Patrick Ausband moved down the road from Duke's Sea Level Hospital in 1990 to become the Harbor's executive director.

Ausband began preparing a feasibility study of a project to aid nonresident seamen in need. Working with Daniel J. Molloy, director of the National Maritime Union's pension and welfare unit, Ausband compiled a trove of background data to support a change of course for the Harbor. Three areas of information were particularly influential in the decision to go ahead with a pilot outreach program:

1. Two-thirds of the men and women eligible for admission to the Harbor were married. Many of the unmarried third were widowed or divorced, and had children or other family ties to a specific area.

2. Seamen had become members of mainstream society through remarkable changes in the work schedule of the maritime industry. Because shipowners want their vessels busy 12 months a year, a single ship must be manned by two sets of masters and crews. For seamen, three or four months at sea earn three or four months with the family. According to Captain Warren G. Leback, former Federal Maritime Administrator writing in the autumn 1996 issue of *Sea History*, able-bodied seamen serving on top-rated ocean vessels earn

$26,000 to more than $29,000 annually, plus benefits, for 32 weeks at sea. A captain's pay is about $110,000 plus benefits for a six-months on, six-months off schedule. Under such circumstances, merchant seamen live in permanent homes and belong to churches and civic organizations, all of which have helped them to develop a sense of roots.

3. Adequate health-care services for the elderly had become available in virtually every corner of the country, eliminating the need for retired sailors to come to one central location for assistance.

The trust assigned a budget of $50,000 to a 12-month project operating in the New York–New Jersey area. Notices in the National Maritime Union's newsletter reported that an unnamed agency was underwriting a program seeking answers to questions such as how much financial assistance it would take to remedy the problems of households in which monthly expenses outran income. An experienced social worker verified applications. Beginning in December 1992, 22 applicants received income-enhancing stipends. To free the recipients from tax liabilities, payments went directly to service providers or vendors such as utilities, landlords, or grocers.

A Case Study

One participant in the pilot program was a 74-year-old, retired seaman who lived with his wife and grandchild in an apartment in Queens. Total monthly income from Social Security, pension, and food stamps was $1,013. Medicaid covered the child but not the seaman or his wife. Estimated monthly expenses for insurance, rent, utilities, transportation, and food (beyond that paid for with $193 in food stamps) was $1,330, leaving a $327 shortfall. Month by month, the family fell deeper into debt despite modest assistance from their grown children. With one of its larger stipends, the Harbor paid the monthly rent bill of $620. Had the seaman chosen to live at Sea Level, the cost of monthly support would have been $3,000 rather than $620. Annual maintenance for an individual at Sailors' Snug Harbor, or in a similar institution, averaged $36,000.

A one-time $3,000 payment for clothing and bedding to a family of six was the largest test-period stipend.

After the outreach program had been in operation for several months, Rose Dubrof—a noted gerontologist at New York City

University's Hunter College—evaluated the project. She found it to be a compassionate, effective operation. The major seafaring unions quickly endorsed outreach because of the large number of pensioned mariners who were likely to benefit from it. The pilot project was extended.

Change of Course

In December 1995, a petition to the Surrogate Court of the State of New York sought permission to proceed with a full-scale outreach program that might result in the closing of the Sea Level home. One year later, Surrogate Eve Preminger granted the trust freedom to do whatever was appropriate to carry out the objectives of the Randall will.

The decision would bring to an end a long and eventful age for the Harbor while opening a totally different era that, as Matthews said, "will allow the best and most appropriate use of the endowment. We'll be able to help hundreds of mariners rather than a few score." It probably will mean the eventual lease or sale of the Sea Level property, he added. The Reverend Barrie Shepherd, successor in 1992 to John B. Macnab as trustee and pastor of First Presbyterian Church, noted, "Always, there will be some who need nursing home or hospital care. The Harbor will see to their needs in a facility close to their homes."

The surrogate court's decision did not come with a blueprint on how to implement the outreach program. Whatever road the trustees finally chose, residents and employees were told, movement was likely to be slow and methodical. The first step was to get the word out. Visits to the maritime unions resulted in newsletter articles about a new day in the life of Sailors' Snug Harbor. A mailing to more than 200 maritime companies, port authorities, and relief agencies that deal with retired seamen told the outreach story. Speakers from the Harbor were heard on what is a casual merchant-mariner lecture circuit.

Initially, only a few residents inquired about relocation. Most seemed content with life at Sea Level. Doors remained open for new admissions: 18 in the 12 months leading up to the year 2000. At the same time, more residents began asking about the outreach program. Eight signed up for the stipends and moved out of Sea Level.

Under the new system, Randall's largess is being delivered in unexpected places such as the Prospect Park YMCA in Brooklyn, where the Seamen's Church Institute has set up a sort of minor league Sailors' Snug Harbor. Five of the eight members of this Brooklyn crew receive stipends from Sea Level. More romantic is the story of the Englishman who sailed for years on American ships before retiring to Chile with his Chilean wife and Randall stipend. He may be the first of what could become the Harbor's international wing. Once the trustees are satisfied that all eligible mariners in the United States are enrolled, they will consider reaching out to foreign brethren. As Ausband explains, hard times are the usual lot for most old salts in the Philippines, Korea, southeast Asia, Russia, and the former Soviet republics. The eligibility rule calling for five years of service on U.S. ships need not be a problem because it was not part of the Randall will. The shipping industry has always been global; it will remain for future trustees to determine how Captain Randall's Snug Harbor bequest should benefit "old, decrepit and worn out" seamen in times to come.

New Life at the Old Home

Without doubt, the outreach program will bring about a tack in the way of life at the Harbor itself. Something surely will change when an accelerating decline in the mariner population leaves excess empty space in what is a highly desirable facility for retirement living. A way will be found to open the building to such white-collar landsmen as retired teachers, realtors, journalists, and civil service mandarins. Maintenance for seamen who stay on would be underwritten by the trust at a negotiated cost. Such a scenario could be adapted to either a lease or a sale by the retirement and nursing-home operators who are interested in taking over the Sea Level property.

Back Home

Whether the Sea Level property is leased or sold, Harbor headquarters will move back to New York where Ausband and a small staff will manage the new stipends program. In addition, the new quarters will include a room for the board of trustees and space for the Harbor's large collection of maritime art. At this writing, a moving date is probably two years away. Matthews exults, "It's strange to say we couldn't wait to get out of New York and now we can't wait to get back."

Visiting the Cultural Center

More than 20 years after the city set about transforming Sailors' Snug Harbor on Staten Island into the Snug Harbor Cultural Center, the project remained a work in progress.

In the relatively affluent days of 1973, the city paid nearly $10 million for the Harbor's 80 acres and 28 buildings. Three years later, on the brink of bankruptcy for reasons that had little to do with the Staten Island purchase, the new administration of Mayor Abraham Beame struggled to find $82,000 for emergency repair and protective maintenance on its newly incorporated, not-for-profit, historic complex.[3]

The long-simmering fiscal crisis burst into headlines in spring 1975 when another excess of deficit spending and short-term borrowing goaded the banks into a shutdown of city credit. The state government in Albany created the Municipal Assistance Corporation to monitor city finances and to borrow on its behalf with bonds guaranteed by the state.[4] By 1980, another new mayor, Edward Koch, had helped restore the city's financial stability, but the cultural center continued as a low-budget item. Membership and fund-raising drives, volunteers, and varying degrees of support from city and state agencies kept the fiscally starved center alive.

Welcome to the cultural center and some of its nonprofit, rent-paying residents.

Full restoration of the buildings would have cost an estimated $13.2 million, according to a 1976 study by the architectural firm of Prentice & Chan, Ohlhausen. Grounds were splendidly maintained, the study found, but the buildings, while structurally sound in nearly all cases, had been deteriorating for a quarter of a century. To begin with, all needed new roofs, upgraded electrical and mechanical systems, and new exit stairs in fireproof shafts. The music hall, with holes in its floors and fallen plaster, was in bad shape. The recreation hall, chapel, and mortuary needed relatively minor repairs, aside from new roofs. Rehabilitation of the five Greek temples—in varying stages of decay—and the three attached rear dormitories would account for nearly half of the costs.

The Neptune Fountain stands on the great lawn in front of the music hall. It was restored at a cost of $700,000.

Architect Rolf Ohlhausen put the price of emergency and interim work at $40,000. Stabilization to prevent further deterioration of building exteriors would run an additional $750,000. "If the initial sums are found," he told the newly appointed board of directors, "you are putting these buildings in the bank for the future. Interim use means limited use, but you haven't lost the whole thing."[5]

In 1977, a cultural group that did not worry about dilapidated structures—The Staten Island Botanical Garden, Inc.—became the sanctuary's first tenant. Its gift shop would open in the former mortuary. In 1978, the Newhouse Center for Contemporary Art moved into space below the Great Hall, formerly the main reading room in the recreation center.

Building B, future home of the Staten Island Institute of Arts and Sciences.

Barren years stood between the city's conceptualization of the cultural center and further realization of this goal. Allan Weissglass, president of the center from 1980 to 1983 and a board member in following years, recalled this period "as make or break time." Summers were easy. Outdoor concerts by the likes of Tony Bennett; dance recitals and one-act plays; an art show; and tours for influentials such as Kitty Carlisle Hart, Helena Rubinstein, Joseph Papp, and Jacqueline Kennedy Onassis brought attention to the center's possibilities. Winter was a time of testing. There was not enough oil at one point to heat the few buildings open for business. One of the many volunteers, Muriel Silberstein-Storfer, a Staten Island neighbor of the Harbor and a board member of the Metropolitan Museum of Art, remembers shivering through meetings in dimly lit rooms with peeling walls. The center's board had trouble at times meeting the payroll tax for its undersized team of employees.[6]

Turnabout began when Staten Island's state senator John J. Marchi won a $4 million legislative grant for the center. Although Albany grudgingly provided the funds in dribs and drabs, by the mid-1980s a spectacular vaulted space in the Great Hall had been converted into a grand interior showpiece, and one of America's best children's museums had moved into what had been built as a large maintenance center in 1903.

With funds for a proposed veterans' memorial that had been accumulating since shortly after World War II, the landmarked chapel was turned into a charming concert space with honor rolls on the walls for Staten Islanders killed in combat. Renovation now entered a lengthy waiting period, but the city did provide infrastructure funds.

A monetary infusion of $700,000 in 1992, most of it raised privately, restored the elaborate bronze Neptune Fountain that stands in a marble basin on the great lawn fronting the music hall. In 1987 an architectural competition for a plan to restore and expand the 850-seat hall itself was won by Rafael Vinoly, an internationally renowned architect. Under the Vinoly design, the music hall—a contemporary of Carnegie Hall—would retain its Greek Revival facade while being transformed into a modern theater with a fly-tower for sets and scenery, a subterranean lobby, an expanded backstage area, and an outdoor plaza.[7] When cost estimates ballooned from $10 million to $18 million, the project was set aside until the spring of 1997 when the first step of a new three-step rehabilitation got under way.[8] Well ahead of schedule and under its $3.4 million budget, the renovated stage and orchestra level opened in October 1997 with Galt MacDermot's commissioned-for-the-occasion Concerto for Snug Harbor and a thirtieth-anniversary celebration of his musical *Hair*.[9]

The newest addition to the cultural center, in a one-acre plot in the Botanical Garden, is a $10 million gift from New York's Chinese community—a traditional, white-walled, roofed garden enclosing teahouse, pavilions, bridges, and ponds. Called the Scholar's Garden, this replica of Imperial China was built by 40 Chinese craftsmen. A tablet over the entrance reads in red and white Chinese characters, "The Garden Where One Experiences Many Beautiful Things."

In 1994, the original Greek temple was reopened in all its 1833 splendor including a triple-height gallery with stained glass, ceiling murals, and sunlit dome. Building D, immediately to its left, is home to the John A. Noble Collection, a maritime museum and study center. It is one of 19 nonprofit, independent, rent-paying residents of the cultural center. Among the others are the Children's Museum, the Botanical Garden, the Art Lab School, the Walsh Theatrical Dance Center, and the Staten Island Conservatory of Music. The Cultural Center Inc. is landlord, manager, and caretaker of the city-owned site.

Rain and snow poured through the open spaces that once contained skylights in the roof of Building D when it was assigned to the Noble

Collection in April 1992. Promised emergency funds were slow to mate-
rialize, so the collection's volunteers repaired the roof. Erin Urban, director of the collection, estimated that volunteers provided $350,000 worth
of work through the years. Among the missing amenities in Building D
were toilet facilities, and again the volunteers rallied. Brooklyn Union Gas
donated the piping, and the center's trustees contributed a toilet and
sink. A licensed plumber came out of the blue, Urban said, and completed installation in two weeks of free work. Walls were built and painted
by other volunteers who also furnished curtains, rug, and plantings.
Until 2001, when the city's $1.4 million adaptation and restoration pro-
gram was scheduled for completion, Building D opened only for members of its education programs and by appointment.

   Forecasts for the remaining three temples in the row are frustrating.
Building E, to the left of D, is currently used as storage space. Someday

*The Chinese Scholar's
Garden, a collection of
pavilions, bridges, and
ponds, is the cultural
center's newest attrac-
tion. It opened in 1999.*

The right wing of the Greek Revival dormitories was to be the site of the Staten Island Museum. It didn't happen. The boarded windows are not likely to open anytime soon.

it may be turned into a dormitory for international artists-in-residence. The right wing of the row, Buildings B and A, were to have been the site of the Staten Island Museum and centerpiece of the new Snug Harbor. Windows in both buildings have been boarded up for years. Unless local politics change, that situation is not likely to improve anytime soon.

The museum is a division of the Staten Island Institute of Arts and Sciences, a principal player in the campaign to have the city purchase Sailors' Snug Harbor in its entirety. Late in 1975, Staten Island Borough President Robert Connor presented New York Mayor Abraham Beame with an 11-member committee of volunteers who would plan and oversee the development of the cultural center.

Connor formed the committee, in part, as a favor to Captain Leo Kraszeski. At the time, the harbor governor and his old seamen remained in their Staten Island quarters awaiting the overdue completion of their home in North Carolina. As the only executive on the grounds, Kraszeski was besieged with queries about the cultural center that he was not in a position to answer. Beame upgraded the committee into the center's first board of directors. Not one of the new directors was a member of the Staten Island Institute of Arts and Sciences. Judge Holt Meyer, who had been one of Lindsay's chief advisors on Snug Harbor issues, watched the institute's interest dwindle and swing from the cultural center to a campaign to develop a greenbelt through central Staten Island. By the mid-1980s, plans were in the works to move the museum from its cramped quarters on Stuyvesant Place near Borough Hall to the St. George waterfront next to the ferry terminal.[10] Nevertheless, the institute remains a constituent of the cultural center and hopes someday to transform Buildings A and B into gallery space.

Among the Culture Center's new attractions is Connie Gretz's Secret Garden, inspired by Frances Hodgson's beloved children's book. The Gretz garden includes a two-story medieval tower where parents can watch children solve the puzzle of a hedge maze.

Entering Snug Harbor through the landmarked gate on Richmond Terrace, a visitor comes upon graveyard serenity and a mostly empty row of classic buildings. A couple of groundskeepers provide the only sign of life. Stroll past the statue of Captain Randall into the interior grounds and come upon a scene that tingles with comings and goings. Building H, immediately behind the shuttered Building B, is the visitors' center, gift shop, and snack bar. G is occupied by the Newhouse Center. All the buildings appear to have tenants or to be well along in the restoration process, including a row of Victorian cottages that face the perennial and herb gardens. Signs of rehabilitation are everywhere—excavations, construction machinery, and stockpiles of building materials. Adaptation has been considerably more expensive than the 1976 estimate of $13.2 million. Management reports that, with 19 buildings occupied, $23.5 million in work has been completed and another $30 million is in progress, including the restoration of the dock that was the very first structure built at Snug Harbor.[11]

Notes

1. Interview with Daniel Paul Matthews.

2. Interviews with F. Patrick Ausband plus a four-page document used to explain the outreach program to Harbor residents and maritime agencies.

3. The sum of $82,000 for "emergency repairs" was reported in the *Staten Island Advance*, June 6, 1976.

4. Ken Auletta, *The Streets Were Paved with Gold*, pp. 90-1.

5. *Staten Island Advance*, May 21, 1976.

6. Interview with Allan Weissglass.

7. Regarding Vinoly's design, see Paul Goldberger's architecture review, *The New York Times,* July 5, 1987.

8. *Staten Island Sunday Advance*, September 1992.

9. *Staten Island Advance*, October 23, 1997.

10. *SIIAS News*, November-December 1997.

11. Celia Reilly, Snug Harbor Cultural Center.

ON THE BEACH.

Last Will and Testament of the Late Robert R. Randall, Esq.

In the Name of God, Amen. I, Robert Richard Randall, of the seventh ward of the city of New York, being weak in body, but of sound and disposing mind and memory, do make and ordain this my last Will and Testament as follows:

First. I direct all my just debts to be paid.

Secondly. I give unto the legitimate children of my brother, Paul R. Randall, each an annuity or yearly sum of forty pounds, until they respectively attain the age of fifteen years; and in addition thereto, I give to each of the sons of my said brother, the sum of one thousand pounds, to be paid to them as they may respectively attain the age of twenty-one years; and also to each daughter which my said brother may have, the like sum of one thousand pounds each, to be paid to them as they respectively be married.

Thirdly. I give and bequeath unto Betsey Hart, my housekeeper, my gold sleeve buttons, and an annuity or yearly payment of forty pounds, to be paid her in quarterly payments, during her natural life.

Fourthly. I give and bequeath unto Adam Shields, my faithful overseer, my gold watch and the sum of forty pounds, to be paid to him as soon after my decease as conveniently may be.

Fifthly. I also give and bequeath unto Gawn Irwin, who now lives with me, my shoe-buckles and knee-buckles, and also the sum of twenty pounds to be paid immediately after my decease.

Sixthly. As to and concerning all the rest, residue and remainder of my estate, both real and personal, I give, devise and bequeath all the same unto the Chancellor of the State of New York, the Mayor and Recorder of the city of New York, the President of the Chamber of Commerce in the city of New York, the President and Vice-President of the Marine Society of the city of New York, the senior Minister of the Episcopal Church in the said city, and the senior Minister of the Presbyterian Church in the said city; to have and to hold all and singular the rest, residue and remainder of my said real and personal estate, unto them, the said Chancellor of the State of New York, Mayor of the city of New York, the Recorder of the city of New York, the President of the Chamber of Commerce, President and Vice-President of the Marine Society, senior Minister of the Episcopal Church, and senior Minister of the Presbyterian Church in the said city, for the time being, and their respective successors in the said offices, for ever, to, for and upon the uses, trusts, intents, and purposes, and subject to the direction and appointments hereinafter mentioned and declared concerning the same; that is to say, out of the rents, issues and profits of the said rest, residue and remainder of my said real and personal estate, to erect and build upon some eligible part of the land upon which I now reside, an Asylum, or Marine Hospital, to be called "The Sailors' Snug Harbor," for the purpose of maintaining and supporting aged, decrepit and worn-out sailors, as soon as they, my said charity Trustees, or a majority of them, shall judge the proceeds of the said estate will support fifty of the said sailors, and upwards. And I do hereby direct that the income of the said real and personal estate, given as aforesaid to my said charity Trustees, shall for ever hereafter be used and applied for supporting the Asylum or Marine Hospital hereby directed to be built, and for maintaining sailors of the above description therein, in such manner as the said Trustees, or a majority of them, may from time, or their successors in office may from time to time, direct. And it is my intention that the institution hereby directed and created should be perpetual, and that the above-mentioned officers for the time being and their successors, should forever continue and be the governors thereof, and have the superintendence of the same; and it is my will and desire that if it cannot legally be done, according to my above intention by them, without an Act of Legislature, it is my will and desire that they will, as soon as possible, apply for an Act of the Legislature to incorporate them for the purposes above specified. And I do further declare it to be will and intention that the said rest, residue and remainder of my real and personal estate should be, at all events, applied for the uses and purposes above set forth; and it is my desire all courts of law and equity will so construe this, my said Will, as to have the said estate appropriated to the above uses, and that the same should in no case, for want of legal form or otherwise, be so construed as that my relations, or any other persons, should heir, possess or enjoy my property except in the manner and for the uses herein above specified. And, lastly, I do nominate and appoint the Chancellor of the State of New York for the time being at the time of my decease, the Mayor of the city of New York for the time being, the Recorder of the city of New York for the time being, the President of the Chamber of Commerce for the time being, the President and Vice-President of the Marine Society of the city of New York for the time being, the senior Minister of the Episcopal Church in the city of New York, and the senior Minister of the Presbyterian Church in the said city, for the time being, and their successors in office after them, to be the executors of this my last Will and Testament, hereby revoking all former and other Wills, and declaring this to be my last Will and Testament.

In witness whereof I have hereunto set my hand and affixed my seal, the first day of June, in the year of our Lord one thousand eight hundred and one.

Robert Richard Randall.[L.S.]

Signed, sealed, published and declared by the said Testator as and for his last Will and Testament, in the presence of us, who in his presence, at his request, and in the presence of each other, have subscribed our names as witnesses thereto [there being an erasure from the word President to the end of the eleventh line of the second page].

Uriah Burdge
Henry Brevoort
Jonas Humbert

City and County of New York, ss:

Be it remembered, that on the tenth day of July, in the year of our Lord one thousand eight hundred and one, personally came and appeared before David Gelston, Surrogate of said County, Uriah Burdge, Henry Brevoort and Jonas Humbert, all of the said city, and being duly sworn on their oaths, declared that they saw Robert Richard Randall, deceased, sign and seal an instrument in writing, purporting to be the Will of the said Robert Richard Randall, bearing date the first day of June, in the year of our Lord one thousand eight hundred and one (the preceding whereof is a true copy), and heard him publish and declare the same as and for his last Will and Testament; that at the time thereof he, the said Robert Richard Randall, was of sound disposing mind and memory, to the best of the knowledge and belief of them, the deponents; and that their names subscribed as witnesses to the said Will, are of their own proper hands writing, which they respectively subscribed as witnesses here to, in the Testator's presence.

David Gelston.

The preceding is a true copy of the original Will of Robert Richard Randall, deceased, and of the Certificate of the proof thereof.

Sylvanus Miller, Surrogate.

GOOD TIMES/HARD TIMES

F or the most part, average annual income and expense figures have increased over the 167-year span that Sailors' Snug Harbor has cared for old seamen, but some of the years that income and expenses were down were distressing. Approximately 90 percent of Harbor income was spent on building and maintaining the Staten Island home until the 1880s when the Trustees felt compelled to "improve" their Manhattan properties.

	Income	Expenses
1833–1842	$ 35,294	$ 26,427
1863–1872	99,767	100,089
1893–1902	370,399	329,967
1923–1932	1,266,951	1,047,795
1942–1951	1,446,108	1,507,528
1952–1961	1,223,992	1,250,619
1962–1971	1,045,785	1,319,333
1972–1981	1,452,121	1,680,422
1982–1991	2,897,400	2,437,104
1992–Present	3,876,235	3,330,877

BIBLIOGRAPHY

Albion, Robert Greenhalgh. *The Rise of the Port of New York: 1815-1860*. New York: Scribners, 1939.

Alden, John Richard. *The American Revolution*. New York: Harper Torchbooks, 1954.

Auletta, Ken. *The Streets Were Paved with Gold*. New York: Random House, 1979.

Asbury, Herbert. *The Gangs of New York*. New York: Capricorn Books, 1970.

Bailey, Anthony. *New York, N.Y.: An American Heritage Extra*. Special issue of *American Heritage Magazine*, 1968.

Barnes, William Morris. *When Ships Were Ships and Not Tin Pots*. New York: Albert & Charles Boni, 1930.

Barry, Gerald J. *Trinity Church: 300 Years of Philanthropy*. New York: The Hundred Year Association of New York, 1997.

Barth, Gunther. *City of People: Rise of Modern City Culture in Nineteenth Century America*. New York: Oxford University Press, 1980.

Batterberry, Michael, and Ariane Batterberry. *On The Town in New York: The Landmark History of Eating, Drinking, and Entertainments*. New York: Routledge, 1999.

Beard, Rick, and Leslie Cohen Berlowitz, eds. *Greenwich Village: Culture and Counterculture*. New Brunswick, N.J.: Rutgers University Press, 1993.

Berg, A. Scott. *Lindbergh.* New York: G. P. Putnam's Sons, 1998.

Berger, Meyer. *Meyer Berger's New York.* New York: Random House, 1960.

Bernstein, Iver. *The New York City Draft Riots.* New York: Oxford University Press, 1990.

Birmingham, Stephen. *Our Crowd.* New York: Harper & Row, 1967.

Blackman, Elizabeth. *Manhattan for Rent 1785-1850.* Ithaca, N.Y.: Cornell University Press, 1989.

Bobbe, Dorothie. *DeWitt Clinton,* new ed. Port Washington, N.Y.: Ira J. Friedman, Inc., 1962.

Bolster, W. Jeffrey. *Black Jacks: African American Seamen in the Age of Sail.* Cambridge, Mass.: Harvard University Press, 1997.

Bone, Kevin, ed. *The New York Waterfront: Evolution and Building Culture of the Port and Harbor.* New York: The Monacelli Press, 1997.

Boyer, Paul. *Urban Masses and Moral Order in America, 1820-1920.* Cambridge, Mass.: Harvard University Press, 1978.

Brandt, Nat. *The Man Who Tried to Burn New York.* Syracuse, N.Y.: Syracuse University Press, 1986.

Brinnin, John Malcolm. *The Sway of the Grand Saloon: A Social History of the North Atlantic.* New York: Delacourt Press, 1971.

Brown, Milton W. *The Story of the Armory Show.* New York: Abbeville Press, 1988.

Burrows, Edwin G., and Mike Wallace. *Gotham: A History of New York City to 1898.* New York: Oxford University Press, 1999.

Caro, Robert A. *The Power Broker: Robert Moses and the Fall of New York.* New York: Alfred A. Knopf, 1974.

Chidsey, Donald Barr. *American Privateers.* New York: Dodd Mead, 1962.

Churchill, Winston. *History of the English-Speaking Peoples.* 1 vol. Ed. Henry Steele Commanger. New York: Greenwich House, 1983.

Cleres, Christian. *Le Havre-New York.* Paris: Editions Hazen, 1997.

Connable, Alfred, and Edward Silverfarb. *Tigers of Tammany.* New York: Holt, Rinehart and Winston, 1967.

Cowley, Malcolm, and Daniel P. Mannix. *Black Cargoes: A History of the Atlantic Slave Trade.* New York: Viking Press, 1962.

Cudahy, Brian J. *Over and Back: The History of Ferryboats in New York Harbor.* New York: Fordham University Press, 1990.

Dana, Richard Henry, Jr. *Two Years before the Mast.* 1840. New York: Penguin Classics, 1986.

Davis, Charles G. *American Sailing Ships: Their Plans and History.* New York: Dover, 1929.

Delaney, Edmund T. *New York's Greenwich Village.* Barre, Mass.: Barre Publishers, 1968.

Diamonstein, Barbarlee. *Landmarks of New York.* New York: Harry N. Abrams, Inc., 1988.

Dictionary of American Biography. New York: Scribners, 1931.

Dix, Morgan, ed. *A History of the Parish of Trinity Church in the City of New York.* 6 vols. New York: Knickerbocker Press, 1906.

Donnan, Elizabeth. *Documents Illustrative of the History of the Slave Trade to America.* 4 vols. New York: The Carnegie Institution; reprint, New York: Octagon Books, 1969.

Draper, Theodore. *A Struggle for Power: The American Revolution.* New York: Vintage/Random House, 1997.

Dreiser, Theodore. *The Color of a Great City.* New York: Boni & Liveright, 1923.

Dunlop, David. *On Broadway: A Journey Uptown Over Time.* New York: Rizzoli, 1990.

East, Robert, and Jacob Judd, eds. *The Loyalist Americans: A Focus on Greater New York.* Tarrytown, N.Y.: Sleepy Hollow Restorations, 1975.

Edmiston, Susan, and Linda D. Cirino. *Literary New York.* Boston: Houghton Mifflin, 1976.

Ellis, Edward Robb. *The Epic of New York City.* New York: Coward-McCann, 1966.

Federal Writers Project. *A Maritime History of New York.* New York: Doubleday, Doran, 1941.

———. *New York Panorama.* New York: Random House, 1938.

———. *The WPA Guide to New York.* New York: Random House, 1939.

Fish, Stuyvesant. *The New York Privateers: 1756-1763.* New York: George Grady Press, 1945.

Fleming, Thomas. *Liberty! The American Revolution.* New York: Viking, 1997.

Flick, Alexander Clarence. *Loyalism in New York During the American Revolution.* New York: Columbia University Press, 1901.

Folpe, Emily Kies. *It Happened on Washington Square.* Baltimore: Johns Hopkins University Press, 2000.

Foster, R. F. *Modern Ireland: 1600-1972*. London: Penguin Press,1988.

Fuess, Claude Moore. *Daniel Webster.* 2 vols. Boston: Little, Brown and Company, 1930.

Gannon, Michael. *Operation Drumbeat.* New York: Harper & Row, 1990.

Gayle, Margot, and Edmund V. Gillon Jr. *Cast-Iron Architecture in New York.* New York: Dover Publications, 1974.

Geisst, Charles R. *Wall Street: A History*. New York: Oxford University Press, 1997.

Gibson, Charles Dana. *Merchantmen? or Ships of War.* Camden, Maine: Ensign Press, 1986.

Gilfoyle, Timothy J. *City of Eros: New York City Prostitution and the Commercialization of Sex, 1790-1920.* New York: W. W. Norton & Co., 1992.

Gilmartin, Gregory. *Shaping the City: History of the Municipal Art Society*. New York: Clarkson Potter/Publishers, 1995.

Goebel, Julius, ed. *The Law Practice of Alexander Hamilton.* 5 vols. New York: Columbia University Press, 1964-81.

Goldberg, Joseph P. *The Maritime Story: A Study in Labor-Management Relation*s. Cambridge, Mass.: Harvard University Press, 1958.

Goldberger, Paul. *The City Observed: A Guide to the Architecture of Manhattan.* New York: Vintage/Random House, 1979.

Goldstone, Harmon H., and Martha Dalrymple. *History Preserved: A Guide to New York City Landmarks and Historic Distric*ts. New York: Simon and Schuster, 1974.

Green, Martin. *New York 1913: The Armory Show and the Paterson Strike Pageant.* New York: Collier/Macmillan, 1988.

Greenwich Village Historic District Designation Report. Vol. 1. New York: Landmarks Preservation Commission, 1969.

Grey, Peter P. *An Informal History of the New York Chamber of Commerce.* New York: Chamber of Commerce, 1968.

Hamlin, Talbot. *Greek Revival Architecture in America.* New York: Oxford University Press, 1944.

Harlow, Frederick Pease. *The Making of a Sailor. 1928.* Reprint, New York: Dover Publications, 1988.

Harrington, Virginia. *New York Merchants on the Eve of Revolution.* New York: Columbia University Press, 1935.

Harris, Cyril M., ed. *Illustrated Dictionary of Historic Architecture.* New York: McGraw-Hill, 1977; Dover Publications, 1983.

Healey, James C. *Foc's'le and Glory Hole; A Study of the Merchant Seaman and His Occupation.* New York: Oxford University Press, 1936.

Herrick, Cheesman A. *The Founder: Stephen Girard.* Philadelphia: Girard College, 1923.

Hicks, O. W. *Sea Tales from Sailors' Snug Harbor.* Privately printed. 1935.

Hohman, Elmo Paul. *A History of American Merchant Seamen.* Hamden, Conn.: Shoestring Press, 1956.

Horsmanden, Daniel. *The New York Conspiracy.* 1744. Reprint, Boston: Beacon Press, 1971.

Hone, Philip. *Diary.* Ed. Bayard Tuckerman. 1889. Reprint, New York: Dodd, Mead and Co, 1910.

Hughes, Robert. *American Visions: The Epic History of Art in America.* New York: Alfred A. Knopf, 1997.

Jackson, Kenneth, ed. *The Encyclopedia of New York City.* New Haven, Conn.: Yale University Press, 1995.

Janvier, Thomas A. *In Old New York.* New York: Harpers, 1894.

Johnson, Thomas H. *The Oxford Companion to American History.* New York: Oxford University Press, 1966.

Kammen, Michael. *Colonial New York.* New York: Oxford University Press, 1975.

Kasson, John F. *Rudeness and Civility: Manners in Nineteenth-Century Urban America.* New York: Hill & Wang, 1990.

Kessner, Thomas. *Fiorello H. La Guardia and the Making of Modern New York.* New York: McGraw Hill, 1989.

Kouwenhoven, John A. *The Columbia Historical Portrait of New York.* New York: Harper & Row, 1953.

Launitz-Schurer, Leopold S. *Loyal Whigs and Revolutionaries: The Making of the Revolution in New York, 1765-1776.* New York: New York University, 1980.

Leback, Captain Warren G. "Are American Merchant Mariners Overpaid?" *Sea History* 79 (autumn 1996): 82.

Lindbergh, Charles A. *The Spirit of Saint Louis.* New York: Scribner's, 1953.

Literary History of the United States. 4th ed. New York: Macmillan, 1974.

Lockwood, Charles. "The Bond Street Area." *The New York Historical Society Quarterly* 56 (October 1972): 309-20.

———.*Bricks and Brownstones: The New York Rowhouse, 1783-1929.* New York: Abbeville Press, 1972.

———. *Manhattan Moves Uptown.* New York: Barnes & Noble Books, 1976.

Longworth, Thomas. *New York Register and City Directory.* New York: Thomas Longworth, Publisher, 1797-1842.

Lydon, James G. *Pirates, Privateers, and Profits.* Upper Saddle River, N.J.: Gregg Press, Inc., 1970.

———. "Slavery in New York." *William and Mary Quarterly 35* (April 1978): 375-94.

Mack, Edward. *Peter Cooper: Citizen of New York.* New York: Duell, Sloan & Pearce,1949.

May, Henry F. *The End of American Innocence: A Study of the First Years of Our Time, 1912-1917.* New York: Alfred A. Knopf, 1964.

Mayer, Grace. *Once Upon a City.* New York: Macmillan, 1958.

McKay, Richard C. *South Street: A Maritime History of New York.* New York: G. P. Putnam's Sons, 1934.

McManus, Edgar J. *A History of Negro Slavery in New York.* Syracuse, N.Y.: Syracuse University Press, 1966.

McPhee, John. *Looking for a Ship.* New York: Farrar Straus Giroux, 1990.

Melville, Herman. *Moby Dick.* 1851. Reprint, Ware, England: Wordsworth Classics, 1992.

Miller, Kerby A. *Emigrants and Exiles: The Irish Exodus to North America.* New York: Oxford University Press, 1985.

Miller, Terry. *Greenwich Village and How It Got That Way.* New York: Crown, 1990.

Moore, Christopher. *New Amsterdam 1643-1644: Frontier, Farms and Freedom.* New York: Schomburg Center, 1993.

Moore, Margaret. *End of the Road for Ladies' Mile?* New York: Municipal Art Society, 1986.

Morehouse, Clifford P. *Trinity: Mother of Churches.* New York: Trinity Church, 1973.

Morison, Samuel Eliot. *Maritime History of Massachusetts: 1783-1860.* Boston: Houghton Mifflin, 1921.

———. *Oxford History of the American People.* New York: Oxford University Press, 1965.

Morris, Ira K. *Morris' Memorial History of Staten Island.* West New Brighton, Staten Island, N.Y.: Memorial Publishing, 1900.

Morris, Lloyd. *Incredible New York: 1850-1950.* New York: Bonanza

Books, 1951.

Morrone, Francis. *The Architectural Guidebook to New York City.* Salt Lake City, Utah: Gibbs-Smith, 1994.

New York *Directory and Register.* New York: Hodge, Allen and Campbell, 1789-91.

Noble, John A. *The Fight for Sailors' Snug Harbor: Essays and Letters of John A. Noble.* New York: The John A. Noble Collection, Staten Island Cultural Center, 1994.

Oates, Stephen B. *With Malice Toward None: A Life of Abraham Lincoln.* New York: Harper Perennial, 1977.

O'Brien, Patrick. *The Maurites Command.* New York: W. W. Norton & Company, 1977, p. 32.

Pope-Hennessy, James. *Sins of the Fathers: A Study of Atlantic Slavers 1441-1807.* New York: Alfred A. Knopf, 1968.

Pumphrey, Ralph E. *Heritage of American Social Work.* New York: Columbia University Press, 1961.

Purcell, L. Edward. *Who Was Who in The American Revolution.* New York: Facts On File, Inc., 1993.

Ranlet, Philip. *The New York Loyalists.* Nashville: University of Tennessee Press, 1986.

Reynolds, Donald Martin. *The Architecture of New York City.* Rev. ed. New York: John Wiley & Sons, 1994.

Robinson-Lorant, Laurie. *Melville: A Biography.* New York: Clarkson Potter, 1996.

Samuels, Samuel. *From the Forecastle to the Cabin.* New York: Harper & Brothers, 1887.

Seitz, Don C. "A History of Captain Robert Richard Randall's Foundation for the Toilers of the Sea." Unpublished manuscript.

Shepherd, Barnett. *Sailors' Snug Harbor: 1801-1976.* New York: Snug Harbor Cultural Center, 1979.

———. "Sailors' Snug Harbor Reattributed to Minard Lefever." *Journal of the Society of Architectural Historians 35* (May 1976).

Silver, Nathan. *Lost New York.* Boston: Houghton Mifflin Company, 1967.

Simon, Kate. *Fifth Avenue: A Very Social History.* New York: Harcourt Brace Jovanovich, 1978.

Smith, Philip Chadwick Foster. *The Empress of China.* Philadelphia: Philadelphia Maritime Museum, 1984.

Smith, Thomas E. V. *The City of New York in the Year of Washington's Inauguration, 1789.* Riverside, Conn.: Chatham Press, 1889.

Spann, Edward K. *The New Metropolis: New York City 1840-1857.* New York: Columbia University Press, 1981.

Standard, William L. *Merchant Seamen and the Law.* New York: National Maritime Union, 1946.

Stern, Robert A. M., with Gregory Gilmartin and John Montague Massengale. *New York 1900: Metropolitan Architecture and Urbanism 1890-1915.* New York: Rizzoli, 1983.

Stern, Robert A. M., with Gregory Gilmartin and Thomas Mellins. *New York 1930: Architecture and Urbanism between the Two Wars.* New York: Rizzoli, 1987.

Stern, Robert A. M., with Thomas Mellins and David Fishman. *New York 1960: Architecture and Urbanism between the Second World War and the Bicentennial.* New York: The Monacelli Press, 1995.

Steinmeyer, Henry G. *Staten Island: 1524-1898.* Rev. ed. New York: Staten Island Historical Society, 1987.

Still, Bayard. *Mirror for Gotham.* New York: New York University Press, 1956.

Stokes, I. N. Phelps. *Iconography of Manhattan Island 1498-1909.* 6 vols. 1915-28. Reprint, New York: Arno Press, 1967.

Syrell, Harold C., ed. *The Papers of Alexander Hamilton.* 24 vols. New York: Columbia University Press, 1961.

Tattersfield, Nigel. *The Forgotten Trade.* London: J. Cape, 1991.

Tauranac, John. *Essential New York.* New York: Holt, Rinehart and Winston, 1979.

Taylor, Alan. *William Cooper's Town: Power and Persuasion on the Frontier of the Early American Republic.* New York: Vintage Books/ Random House, 1995.

Thomas, Hugh. *The Slave Trade.* New York: Simon & Schuster, 1997.

Tomkins, Calvin. *Merchants and Masterpieces: The Story of the Metropolitan Museum of Art.* New York: E. P. Dutton & Co., 1970.

Trow, John F. *Trow's New York City Directory.* New York: Trow Publishing, 1866-1925.

Tsouras, Peter. *Gettysburg: An Alternative History.* Mechanicsburg, Penn.: Stackpole Books, 1997.

Turner, Justin G., and Linda Levitt Turner. *Mary Todd Lincoln: Her Life and Letters.* New York: Alfred A. Knopf, 1972.

Valentine, D. T. *Manual of the Corporation of New York.* New York: Edmund Jones & Co., Printers, 1858, 1864, 1865, 1866.

Valentine's Manual of Old New York. Ed. Henry Collins Brown. New York: Valentine's Manual Inc., 1926.

von Pressentin Wright, Carol. *Blue Guide: New York.* New York: W. W. Norton & Co., 1991.

Ware, Caroline F. *Greenwich Village: 1920-1930.* New York: Harper Colophon Books, 1935.

Warner, Amos G. *American Charities.* 4th ed. New Brunswick, N.J.: Transaction Publishers, 1930.

Waters, Frank. *Eight Bells: Sailors' Snug Harbor Yarns and Ballads.* New York: D. Appleton & Co., 1927.

Watson, John F. *Annals and Occurrences of New York City and State in the Olden Time.* Philadelphia: Henry F. Anners, 1846.

Willensky, Elliot, and Norval White. *AIA Guide to New York City.* 3rd ed. New York: Harcourt Brace Jovanovich, 1988.

Wilson, James Grant, ed. *The Memorial History of the City of New York.* 4 vols. New York: New York History Company, 1893.

Wolfe, Gerald R. *New York: A Guide to the Metropolis.* 2nd ed. New York: McGraw Hill, 1994.

Picture Credits

Frontispiece: Michael Wolfe, Wilmington, N.C.

P. 1: New York Public Library, Mid-Manhattan Picture Collection

P. 3: M.A. Hardin Collection

P. 4: Collection of the New-York Historical Society #46215

P. 7: Collection of the New-York Historical Society #46495

P. 9: Collection of the New-York Historical Society #6211

P. 13: Valentine's Manual 1865, page 640

P. 23: Collection of the New-York Historical Society #28666

P. 24: The First Presbyterian Church, New York City

P. 26: Collection of Sailors' Snug Harbor

P. 29: Sepp Seitz, New York

Pp. 30, 31: Milstein Division of U.S. History, Local History and Genealogy, The New York Public Library, Astor, Lenox and Tilden Foundations

P. 36: M.A. Hardin Collection

Pp. 37–38: Sepp Seitz, New York

P. 41: Collection of the Staten Island Institute of Arts and Science

P. 42: Fairfield Aerial Survey, 1936, Collection of Sailors' Snug Harbor

P. 47: Painting by Joseph William Burgess, ASMA, 1998, New York

P. 48: Milstein Division of U.S. History, Local History and Genealogy, The New York Public Library, Astor, Lenox and Tilden Foundations

P. 50: *New York Illustrated*, circa 1860, New York University Archives

Pp. 53 and 55: New York University Archives

P. 57: William James Bennett, after John William Hill. I. N. Phelps Stokes Collection, Miriam and Ira D. Wallach Division of Art, Prints and Photographs, The New York Public Library, Astor, Lenox and Tilden Foundations

P. 59: Museum of the City of New York, Print Archives

P. 61: Museum of the City of New York, Byron Collection

P. 63: Museum of the City of New York, Gift of Harry Shaw Newman 43.368.2

P. 64: Collection of the New-York Historical Society #37036

P. 64: Peter Cooper photo by Sarony. Collection of the New-York Historical Society #44608

P. 66: Lith. Serrell and Perkins, circa 1850, Museum of the City of New York. Gift of Karl Schmidt/37.361.423

P. 68: Collection of the New-York Historical Society #1283

P. 75: Collection of Sailors' Snug Harbor

P. 79: M.A. Hardin Collection

Pp. 82, 84: Sepp Seitz, New York

P. 85: Collection of the Staten Island Institute of Arts and Science,
    photo by Eric Aerts

Pp. 86, 87, 89, 90, 92, 93: Byron, N.Y., M.A. Hardin Collection

P. 94: Snug Harbor Cultural Center Collection

Pp. 95, 96, 98: Collection of Sailors' Snug Harbor

P. 100: The Parish of Trinity Church in the City of New York

P. 109: Collection of the New-York Historical Society #43708

P. 111 Milstein Division of U.S. History, Local History and Genealogy,
    The New York Public Library, Astor, Lenox and Tilden Foundations

P. 112: Collection of the New-York Historical Society, 1887, #43389

P. 115: Elmer MacRae Papers, Collection Archive, Hirshhorn Museum
    and Sculpture Garden, Smithsonian Institution. Gift of the Joseph
    H. Hirshhorn Foundation, 1966

P. 115: The Tamiment Institute Library, New York University

P. 117: Collection of the New-York Historical Society #58885

P. 118: Museum of the City of New York, circa 1908, Byron Collection

P. 119: Milstein Division of U.S. History, Local History and Genealogy,
    The New York Public Library, Astor, Lenox and Tilden Foundations

P. 121: Sepp Seitz, New York

P. 125: Collection of the New-York Historical Society #58522

P. 127: Museum of the City of New York, Print Archives

P. 132: Andreas Feininger, 1943. Collection of the New-York Historical
    Society #67650

P. 137: Museum of the City of New York, Print Archives

P. 142: The First Presbyterian Church, New York City

P. 144: Collection of the Staten Island Institute of Arts and Sciences

P. 145: The John A. Nobel Collection, Snug Harbor Cultural Center

P. 149: Collection of Sailors' Snug Harbor

P. 151: from William Dow

P. 152: Snug Harbor Cultural Center Archives

Pp. 153, 157: Sepp Seitz, New York

Pp. 160, 162, 163, 164, 165, 166, 167: Michael Wolfe, Wilmington, N.C.

P. 170: The Parish of Trinity Church in the City of New York

P. 171: Michael Wolfe, Wilmington, N.C.

Pp. 175, 176, 177, 179, 180: Sepp Seitz, New York

P. 181: Christina Rubin, Brooklyn, N.Y.

P. 183: M.A. Hardin Collection

INDEX

About the Author

Gerald J. Barry has been a newspaperman in Detroit, New England, London, England, and New York City. He wrote for *Newsweek* for eight years before joining a large international firm as its first director of publications. Since his retirement, he has been studying and writing about the history of New York City and of Greenwich Village. He is the author of the *Marine Society of the City of New York, 1770-1995* and *Trinity Church: 300 Years of Philanthropy.*

13644691R00135

Made in the USA
Lexington, KY
11 February 2012